MURDER

IN THEIR HEARTS

In the early twentieth century this site was identified as the location of Chief Logan's camp. Today it is in the middle of farm fields.

MURDER
IN THEIR HEARTS

DAVID THOMAS MURPHY

THE FALL CREEK MASSACRE

Indiana Historical Society Press | Indianapolis, 2010

Printed in the United States of America

This book is a publication of the
Indiana Historical Society Press
Eugene and Marilyn Glick Indiana History Center
450 West Ohio Street
Indianapolis, Indiana 46202-3269 USA
www.indianahistory.org
Telephone orders 1-800-447-1830
Fax orders 1-317-234-0562
Online orders @ http://shop.indianahistory.org

The paper in this publication meets the minimum requirements of American National
Standard for Information Sciences—Permanence of Paper for Printed Library Materials,
ANSI Z39. 48–1984

Library of Congress Cataloging-in-Publication Data

Murphy, David Thomas, 1960–
Murder in their hearts : the Fall Creek massacre / David Thomas Murphy.
    p. cm.
Includes bibliographical references and index.
ISBN 978-0-87195-285-1 (pbk. : alk. paper) 1. Madison County (Ind.)—Race relations—
History—19th century. 2. Massacres—Indiana—Madison County—History—19th century.
3. Indians of North America—Violence against—Indiana—Madison County—History—19th
century. 4. Pioneers—Indiana—Madison County—History—19th century. 5. Whites—
Indiana—Madison County—History—19th century. 6. Frontier and pioneer life—Indiana—
Madison County. 7. Trials (Murder)—Madison County—History—19th century. 8. Madison
County (Ind.)—Race relations—Political aspects—History—19th century. 9. Madison County
(Ind.)—Biography. 10. Madison County (Ind.)—History—19th century. I. Title.
F532.M2M87 2010
305.8009772'57–dc22
                    2010000174

*To the memory of Rosemary Hoehne Murphy, and
to her grandchildren, Madeline, Xavier, Julian, Gilbert,
Isabel, Mathilda, and Eleanor, who miss her very much.*

Contents

Acknowledgments

The story of the Fall Creek Massacre could not have been written without the assistance of many individuals and institutions. I owe special thanks to the following: Professors J. Douglas Nelson and Carl Caldwell of Anderson University; Janet Brewer, Jill Branscum and the staff of the Nicholson Library at Anderson University; Indiana Historical Society Press editors Paula Corpuz, Kathleen Breen, and Ray Boomhower, and the staff of the Indiana Historical Society library, for their assistance in navigating through the Society's rich collection; Andy Hite, the site manager of John Johnston's estate at the Piqua Historical Site in Piqua, Ohio, who generously shared his time and insight into Johnston's career; the staff of the Ohio Historical Society at Columbus; Beth Oljace and the staff of the Indiana Room at the Anderson Public Library; Drew Wilson, whose paper in my Historical Inquiry class first drew my attention to the Fall Creek Massacre; Marcia Martin Murphy, whose comments reshaped and improved many aspects of the finished work; the staff of the Indiana State Archives in Indianapolis; the staff of the Indiana State Library; and the faculty of Anderson University, who provided financial support in a faculty development grant, a Falls Fund Distinguished Scholar grant, as well as a sabbatical leave of absence to complete the writing of the manuscript.

Introduction

"My conclusions have cost me some labour from the want of coincidence between accounts of the same occurrences by different eye-witnesses, arising sometimes from imperfect memory, sometimes from undue partiality for one side or the other."[1]

THUCYDIDES

In the first six months of 1825, three white men were sentenced to death and hanged in Madison County, Indiana. During the previous spring, the trio had incited a gang of angry settlers to the premeditated murder of nine Indians camped along a tributary of Fall Creek where it flows through the county. At the time, the killings and the executions that followed sparked a national sensation. The slaughter in the soggy Indiana creek bottoms created a short-lived but serious national security crisis, and the affair retains a significance that transcends the local.

General histories of the pioneer era, when they note the Fall Creek Massacre at all, usually do so only in passing, although some appreciation of the massacre's legacy lives on in central Indiana. These incidents once inspired a novel by Jessamyn West, an Indiana Quaker. The living history museum at Conner Prairie, near Indianapolis, sometimes stages trial reenactments for the benefit of students and local history buffs. Motorists passing through rural Madison County near the village of Markleville can still find a weathered bronze historical marker on the north shoulder of Indiana State Road 38, a long mile of cornfields, creeks, and woods southeast of the massacre site.

But the events at Fall Creek merit a larger place than they are typically accorded in the national memory of the era as well.[2] Quite apart from any deeper historical significance, the dramatic story of that bloody spring remains gripping in and of itself. The carnage perpetrated by the white settlers, recounted in lurid detail in the contemporary press, retains a shocking impact into the present day. And, while violence between settlers and Native Americans was not unusual in the Old Northwest Territory during the early nineteenth century, this particular incident provoked a fateful and most unusual reaction. White men responsible for the outrage were singled out and hunted down, brought to trial, convicted by a jury of their neighbors, and, for the first

Between 1803 and 1809 Indiana territorial governor William Henry Harrison negotiated a series of land-cession treaties that opened the territory to settlement, causing unrest among the Native Americans. In 1810 Tecumseh warned Harrison against further land cessions, noting "you have taken our lands from us and I do not see how we can remain at peace with you if you continue to do so."

time under American law, sentenced to death and executed for the murder of Native Americans.

Those murders, and the subsequent executions, are also edifying for the student of history, and of American history in particular. There may be few historically verifiable incidents that remain more closely veiled in the fog with which time and frail human memory surround our past. Madison County lost its first courthouse (it is now on its third) to fire in 1880. Documents relevant to the accurate imposition of land taxes miraculously survived, but the blaze appears to have destroyed most of the early court records, including the original transcripts of the Fall Creek trials.

Information on the murders and their aftermath must be culled from a few surviving, mostly incidental sources—fragmentary redactions of the legal proceedings, one published confession, a bare handful of dubious newspaper articles, scanty official correspondence, and the faulty memoirs set down decades later by participants in and witnesses to the proceedings. These have left a maddeningly blurred and ambiguous record. What historian Carl Waldman noted of Native American history in general—"hearsay and legend play a part in what has been passed down. Contradictions abound."—finds in this case a vivid specific instance.[3]

What, exactly, happened at Fall Creek? That depends upon whom you ask. Beyond the elementally irreducible fact of violent death, virtually every meaningful aspect of the answer is subject to dispute. Did nine, or did ten, Indians inhabit the camp that was attacked? Were they mixed-race, Shawnee, Miami, Seneca, Delaware, Wyandotte, or even, in the case of one victim, white? Were five, six, or seven white men in the group that raided the camp and killed its inhabitants? Which of the murderers killed which of the victims? What did the accused murderers say, and what did local inhabitants and state officials do in response to the killings?

For all these questions, and for a great many more, the sources provide multiple and often conflicting answers. Take a single striking example. The date of the killings, which occurred on Monday, March 22, 1824, according to all other accounts—reports appeared in newspapers at the end of that very week—is noted incorrectly not once, but twice, as April 20, 1824, in the official documents filed by Moses Cox, Madison County's bluff, hearty, but not particularly competent first court clerk.[4]

Fall Creek remains memorable as well for the searing case study it affords in the tragic dynamics of relations between the native tribes and white settlers on the American frontier. The volatile and combustible mix of human shortcomings that so often plagued European America's collision with Native Americans—mutual incomprehension, race hatred, greed, violence, and land hunger—exploded with shattering force in the woods around Fall Creek. And as is usually the case in such affairs, the historian must struggle to find an authentic historical voice for the nonliterate native victims of the advancing white society. They left no contemporary written records, took no active part in the legal proceedings, and were banished from the lands where these crimes occurred. Not only their tribal identities, but their very names, in most cases, are lost to history. What they contribute to the memory of these events comes through the eyes and written records of members of an encroaching alien society, some of whom romanticized and others of whom vilified the strangers about whom they wrote.

The bloodshed at Fall Creek also has a particular poignancy for thoughtful observers of global history at the dawn of the twenty-first century. In the midst of a catastrophic epoch of forced migration, population transfers, genocide, and ethnic cleansing in the West and around the world, it is useful to reflect on the origins and aftermath of this particular episode of interethnic violence. Like a tremor shaking the earth's crust where plates scrape past one another, the massacre erupted along one of the fault lines where two massive, somewhat haphazard, migrations collided. One of these was the scattering of European Americans westward across the continent from its eastern and southeastern fringes. The other was the fitful, forced westward retreat of the native peoples.

These popular migrations in the heart of North America, in turn, were a part of the vast global reshuffling of peoples that has characterized the entire modern era. Wherever they occurred, from southern Africa to central Asia to North America and elsewhere, large-scale human relocations generated friction. Often, violence erupted. Governments typically either ignored or actively aided and abetted such bloodshed. In this particular case, however, the demographic upheaval that inflicted predictable suffering on an isolated frontier community also provoked an unusual, decisive, and bloody intervention, in the name of justice, by the State.

Modern Americans may experience a seductive temptation to view the Fall Creek story as a reassuring proof of our nation's judicial equity. Here, many may feel, is a shining exception in a generally sordid record of legal relations between whites and Indians—"a just tribute to the impartial execution of our laws," as Lewis Cass, governor of the Michigan Territory, put it in 1826.[5]

While entirely understandable, such an interpretation probably does violence to the motives of most of those involved and to the actual historical significance of what occurred. It is hard to say how well "justice" in any abstract sense was here served. Some of the white killers—poor, marginalized, bitter, and victimized by appalling racial violence—were clearly stunned to find that they would be called to account to satisfy the newfound moral scruples of a state that normally winked at such bloodshed. While both guilty and brutal, and by the standards of their day deserving of their destined punishment, these frontiersmen found themselves ground in a mill whose relentless workings they could only dimly perceive. In their wretchedness and hatred, they seem at times as pitiable as their victims.

The encouragement of economic growth and the preservation of regional security, in any case, were at least as important to the prosecution of the murderers as was any high-minded commitment to justice for the victims. Still, although mundane material considerations moved the stern and impartial hand of justice, the governments of Indiana and the United States, to give them due credit, were undoubtedly determined to maintain the fragile peace of interracial coexistence by finding a kind of equity. Their success in doing so proved to be merely local, temporary, and imperfect. Nonetheless, the aftermath of the massacre helps to illuminate the complex interaction between popular values and a commitment to the rule of law that permits social stability to emerge from ethnic and economic transformation.

It is likely that the implications of the Fall Creek Massacre for this last element—the rule of law—have something to do with its eclipse from national memory. Nations, like individuals, are typically more at ease celebrating their triumphs than they are conceding their failures. It is as a reminder of unrealized ideals, rather than as a victory of justice, that Fall Creek must stand. If the apprehension and punishment of the murderers had really signaled a new beginning, a landmark precedent for the extension of equal justice under the rule of law, it might today be commemorated as a glorious breakthrough in the jurisprudence of American-native relations. The retribution here meted out in defense of Indian lives, however, failed to establish a new norm as America continued its push westward into the lands of tribal peoples. Instead, Fall Creek remained an anomaly, a stillborn precedent, more comfortably forgotten than recalling Americans, perhaps, to an unsettling awareness of how frequently our practical pursuit of justice fell short of our best aspirations.

1

Slaughter: The Morning of March 22, 1824

"The most terrifying reflection (I am speaking now for myself) is that all these people are not the product of the exceptional but of the general— of the normality of their place, and time, and race." [1]

JOSEPH CONRAD

The Indians probably detected the approach of strangers long before the seven white men finally stepped out of the woods and into their camp. Many signs warned of their impending presence. For one thing, the spring of 1824 was even wetter than normal in central Indiana. Deer Lick Creek, where Chief Logan and his band had pitched their winter settlement, was usually a trickle that drained into Fall Creek before descending to the White River. Now it was swollen with the heavy rain that had fallen overnight and into the morning. The downfall saturated the thick-soiled forest of maple, sycamore, beech, and hickory in the valley of the White River, flooding the wilderness and turning much of it into a waterlogged swamp. Even if the white men made an attempt at stealth, which seems unlikely since they had been drinking heavily for some days, the splashing and sloshing of seven pairs of feet winding their way through the trees would have been audible. In addition to the conditions and to the drink, the dogs that lived with the Indians raised a din whenever strangers neared the camp. [2]

Later, some of the white men recalled that the presence of intruders at their camp made the Indians visibly uneasy, which is not surprising given that only two Indian men faced the seven whites. The small band of Indians—three men, three women, two adolescent boys, and two younger girls—had set up camp in the thinly settled wilds of Madison County four months earlier to hunt, trap, gather furs, and boil maple sugar when the sap rose in the spring. On this soggy Monday morning, only the Indian men known to the whites as Logan and Ludlow remained by the fires and kettles of the camp. The third, M' Doal, was out on the forest trails, checking his network of traps for raccoons and other fur-bearing animals. So, the white men outnumbered the Indians by more than three to one. They may also have been intimidating for another reason—they were heavily armed. Some carried butchers' knives, and each bore a Kentucky rifle, the lethal, long-barreled flintlock that was a frontier staple through the early 1830s.[3]

At least some of the whites, possibly all, were known to the Indians. In certain cases, prior acquaintance might have been a good thing, tending to put the Indians at their ease and reduce tension. This was not such a case. Their knowledge of these particular whites may have been partly to blame for the anxiety displayed by Ludlow and Logan. The Indians had traded actively with the small population of white frontier families, and though later sources customarily describe their band as "friendly," "orderly," and "inoffensive," contemporary testimony suggests that there was at least some friction.[4] Two of the white men, James Hudson and Thomas Harper, were known to have visited and traded with the Indians.

Hudson later accused Ludlow of threatening to kill white men for disturbing his traps. Rumor in the county also had it that the same Ludlow, in a drunken rage, drew his knife and threatened Phebe Hudson, James's wife, when she refused to exchange maple sugar for an Indian basket.[5] Although these claims may have been no more than ex post facto rationalizing, they are not at all implausible. Given the climate of mutual suspicion that often prevailed between whites and Indians, and the occasional influence of liquor, it is easy to suppose that in their four-month stay some of the Indians may have quarreled with whites over trade or property.

Peaceful, wary coexistence, however, seems to have been the norm between these Indians and most of the tiny, widely scattered settler community in Madison County. Now, the newly arrived white men, led by Harper and Hudson, quickly took advantage of this generally harmonious climate to dispel suspicion. Harper stepped forward and shook Ludlow's hand. Then the newcomers spent some time—"until our clothes were dried and our bodies warmed"—lounging by the fires, talking with the Indian men.[6] In the course of their conversations, Ludlow grew petulant, complaining that some whites had stolen a dog he bought from Harper. The issue was dropped without argument, however, when Harper and Andrew Sawyer made an offer to Ludlow and Logan. Two of Sawyer's mares, extremely valuable property, had run off: Would the Indians accompany the men into the forest to help in their recovery?

Ludlow initially seemed reluctant. "May be, if I go, I shoot white man."

But after being offered the substantial fee of fifty cents apiece—a goodly sum, when land in the county could be had at the price of $1.25 an acre—both men accepted the money and prepared to follow the whites into the woods. Logan took a knife. Ludlow armed himself with a knife, a gun, and a tomahawk.[7]

The group, now nine in number, set off into the forest. Picking their way through the trees for about a mile to the southwest, they reached an abandoned cabin at a site the local settlers called "the Big Lick." Here a number of mineral springs rose and meandered into Deer Lick Creek, washing over rocks in a shallow, briny basin that left a coating of salt, lime, sulfur, and iron. These mineral deposits attracted an abundance of animals, making the swampy bottomlands an attractive hunting and trapping ground with which the Indians were as familiar as the whites.[8] Most of the white men—Harper, Sawyer, his fifteen-year-old son, Stephen, seventeen-year-old James Bridge, and Andrew Jones—retired into the cabin. Hudson waited outside, in company with the Indians and eighteen-year-old John T. Bridge Jr., the brother of James.

While the men in the cabin talked and drank, Ludlow passed the time by testing his marksmanship in shooting at a duck. His weapon, though, "snapped," the flint failing to ignite the priming charge that was meant to spark the propellant in the rifle barrel. This was a common mishap, one that was almost predictable given the continued drizzle in the already-soggy forest. A few minutes later, the rest of the white men emerged from the cabin, bringing their bottles and offering to drink whiskey with the Indians. Logan declined. Ludlow, on the other hand, drank eagerly, and all the men but Logan shared several rounds of the potent liquor.

After drinking for some time, the men left the site of the cabin to go deeper into the forest, separating into two groups. Logan accompanied Hudson, Jones, and Bridge Jr. Ludlow set off in a different direction with Harper, the two Sawyers, and a new white man, John T. Bridge Sr., the father of the two Bridge boys and Harper's brother-in-law. Young James Bridge, for reasons never made clear—dread, perhaps, at anticipation of coming events—left the group. The two bands of armed men, a single Indian in each, slowly wandered another half mile or so farther into the woods of the Big Lick, out of sight of one another and of the Indian camp, but within hearing range.

As Logan's party moved on, his three white companions gradually drifted back, dropping twenty yards or so behind the elderly Indian. Bridge Jr. and Jones spoke hurriedly with Hudson. Somewhere in the distant woods, a gunshot boomed. Jones and Bridge Jr. immediately raised their rifles, took aim at Logan's exposed back, and pulled their triggers. Both guns misfired. Hudson's luck was better. Before Logan could turn, he raised his rifle and fired into the Indian's back. The massive leaden slug, nearly a half inch in diameter and weighing half an ounce, blasted Logan's body at point blank range with explosive force, piercing his back and exiting his chest, leaving a gaping hole.

Court records state that Logan died instantly. Hudson, however, recalled that still standing, with blood pouring from both sides of his body, he turned and screamed—"You kill me!" Bridge Jr. dashed forward and rammed Logan in the chest with the stock of his rifle. The Indian buckled into a sitting position on the ground. Jones, his rifle now recharged, stepped up to the sitting Logan and thrust the muzzle of his weapon to within a few inches of the helpless man's face. Covering his eyes with his hands, Logan begged, "If you shoot me, shoot me through the head." Jones tried to oblige, pulling the trigger. His weapon again misfired. Bridge Jr. strode forward, clubbed his rifle, and struck Logan's head.

Logan, probably already dead, lay stretched supine, unmoving and unconscious. Bridge joined Hudson a few steps away, where both men worked frantically to reload. Losing patience, Hudson urged Bridge Jr. to put the old man "out of his misery." Young Bridge dropped his rifle, drew a nine-inch butcher's knife, and drove it twice through Logan's chest. The trio then dragged their victim's broken, bloody corpse into the flooded cavity left by a fallen tree, hiding it hastily in the damp muck beneath the roots.

Ludlow, Logan's truculent companion, was already dead. The gunshot that signaled Hudson's party to murder Logan had been Ludlow's death knell, cutting him down with the same cold-blooded calculation that claimed Logan's life. When his party set off into the woods, Harper led the way. Just as Hudson had done with Logan, Harper gradually fell behind to join the other white men. The unsuspecting Ludlow was left alone, walking with his back turned to his four white companions. After traveling for some distance in this way, Harper stopped. As the other whites watched, he paused, took deliberate aim, and discharged the rifle into Ludlow's exposed back. The Indian fell on his face, dead, it was said, before he hit the ground. None of Harper's companions fired. The fate of Ludlow's corpse is unknown.

Both bands of killers then reassembled at Sawyer's nearby farmstead. Their day's work was just beginning. Harper, Sawyer, and Bridge Sr. were determined to complete the destruction. M' Doal, the women, and the children, they insisted, also had to be killed. At their urging, the other men reloaded their rifles and set off to return to the Indians' camp.

Their brutality had taken a psychic toll on some of the settlers, though. Like new soldiers shaken by bloodshed in the wake of their first battle, some members of the murderous band succumbed to an emotional crisis after the psychological exertion of the killings. They faltered, lost direction, and sank into depression and lassitude, apparently incapacitated by a dawning awareness of the magnitude of their brutality. Hudson, head in hands, crouched on a stump, refusing to proceed. Bridge Jr. also felt stunned and disoriented by his own deeds. Slowing on the path, he turned aimlessly, telling the older man that he wanted no part of any further killing.

Hudson's defection from their band evoked little response. The youth's emotional collapse, on the other hand, infuriated his accomplices. Bridge Jr.'s

The site known as Big Lick in 1824 as it appears in the present day.

uncle, Harper, reminded him angrily that Indians had killed members of his own family during the War of 1812, including his "brave uncle." Bridge Sr., the boy's father, exasperated by what he clearly felt was his son's loss of nerve, taunted him for "cowardice," cited Scripture, and reminded him that "God commanded us to kill our enemies." As other men in the group joined in the chastisement, the pressure of his peers took effect. Slowly regaining his composure, the boy dropped his objections and continued on to the Indian camp.[9]

With Hudson remaining behind, the six white men strode into the midst of the wigwams at a measured walk. All three Indian women, naturally alarmed by the sound of distant gunfire and the return of the whites without Ludlow and Logan, rushed to meet them. One of the women, later described in some accounts as being of mixed white and Delaware heritage, spoke some broken English. Stepping forward in agitation, she asked what had happened to the Indian men. Momentarily shamed and lost for words, the guilty whites muttered that Logan and Ludlow would soon return.

Then, as the woman turned excitedly aside, Bridge Sr. raised his rifle and fired into her back. She sank to her knees, bleeding, but alive and begging for mercy in the name of Jesus and for the sake of their shared white blood. In answer, one of the men dashed in her skull with a hominy pounder, a long, weighty wooden maul. Sawyer shot one of the other women. Bridge Jr., all scruples apparently overcome, killed the last of the women.

Four stunned and defenseless children now faced the monsters who had murdered their parents. There is no record of whether they attempted to escape. None did. Wielding knives, tomahawks, and rifles, the whites slaughtered all four. When the shooting and slashing finally ceased, Sawyer noticed that one of the boys was still moving. Seizing the youth by his ankles, the squat, powerfully built Sawyer, a strong, healthy man of about thirty-five, swung the boy through the air and dashed his brains out against the butt end of a fallen log.

As the gory frenzy subsided, M' Doal stumbled back into the edge of the camp, loaded with animal carcasses collected during his rounds checking traps. Like the women, he had been alarmed by the sound of distant gunfire. Seeing the shambles at the camp, the horrified Indian dropped his catch and turned to flee. At least one of the men, possibly two, opened fire. Though some of the whites believed he was struck by one of the gunshots, there is no conclusive evidence of this. M' Doal survived at least long enough to bolt from the slaughter at the camp. The only Indian to escape this massacre, he was last seen fleeing into the forest.

Perhaps the whites stood for a moment in silence, surrounded by the broken victims of their fury. If so, they did not remain immobile for long. Taking knives, tomahawks, and clubs, the men systematically mutilated the corpses of the women and children, stabbing, beating, and hacking some of the bodies into pieces, with the evident intent of making the deaths seem the result of crazed or drunken violence perpetrated by the Indian men themselves. When finished with this gruesome butchery—"the earth was covered with blood, brains and mangled pieces of human flesh!" Hudson remembered—Harper, Bridge Sr., and the others stripped the seven corpses and heaped them in a nearby "hog wallow," a muddy depression in the forest that was flooded into a pond by the heavy rains.[10]

The removal of the disfigured corpses to the wallow was followed by a thorough looting of the Indians' camp. Cupidity as much as race hatred, in fact, later emerged as one of the prime motives driving Harper, a catalyst of the massacre and probably the most insistent and bitter enemy of the Indians that morning. Logan and his band had amassed a good deal of portable wealth during their stay in Madison County. The fur trade in central and northern Indiana was reaching its zenith in the early 1820s. Harper on an earlier visit had noted the collection of valuable skins—probably raccoon, muskrat, and mink for the most part—in and around the wigwams at Ludlow and Logan's camp.

The Indian men and their wives had also accumulated a considerable store of goods derived from, and created for, their lively trade with the white community. These included the valuable brass kettles used in the boiling of maple sugar, as well as many so-called Indian goods—broadcloth, blankets, fringed deerskin leggings, embroidered and beaded moccasins, etched knives, and much more. Such items were not easily obtained and of considerable worth in areas such as Madison County that were somewhat removed from well-traveled routes of commerce. The white men took all they could, stripping the camp of items that might be useful or valuable in barter.

The robbery of the slaughtered Indian band concluded the sustained depravity begun that morning. The time, by now, had reached the middle or latter half of the afternoon. Although some of the killers were beginning to worry about detection, most seem to have believed that, once their crimes were discovered, they would be able to divert suspicion from themselves. It is also likely, to judge from a later witness, that they accurately sensed that many in the white community would not judge their actions to be criminal. In any event, the band of men separated once more into two groups and began to return home. Hudson followed the two Sawyers to their nearby log cabin. The other killers returned to the Bridge farm. Perhaps they thought, as they turned their backs on their apparently lifeless victims, that the violence was now behind them.

Map of Indiana and Ohio in the 1820s.

Fort Wayne

INDIANA

Pendleton

MADISON CO.

Indianapolis

Vincennes

Corydon

Lewis Town

Piqua

OHIO

BUTLER CO.

HAMILTON CO.

STACY SIMMER

2

"Into the deep and silent forest"
Native Life behind the Northwest Frontier

"The social tie, which distress had long since weakened, is then dissolved; they have lost their country, and their people soon desert them; their very families are obliterated; the names they bore in common are forgotten, their language perishes, and all traces of their origin disappear."[1]

ALEXIS DE TOCQUEVILLE

The families who followed Chief Logan to Madison County in that fall of 1823 probably did not think of themselves as part of a dying breed. Elegiac tones seem to come naturally when writing the history of whites and Indians in America—there is much to lament—but this obscures the historical reality of native experience. The vanishing of races and the passing of peoples, those mournful themes that echo across the literature and history of Native Americans from the era of Alexis de Tocqueville and James Fennimore Cooper to the present, did not seem very applicable to backwoods Indiana in the early 1820s. The Indians were still a vital immediate presence, numbering in the thousands, efficient at meeting their own needs, capable of waging bloody war, and certainly in a position to pursue traditional ways of life that challenged the dominance of the white-settler community, at least for the time being.[2]

Many Americans have long found it convenient to conceive the history of the native peoples after the arrival of Europeans as one long sunset. This was so as long ago as the 1840s, when Indiana pioneers such as John Dillon waxed sentimental about the once-powerful Miami, "slowly tottering towards the grave of their nation."[3] This, however, imparts to our shared history a comforting and misleading sense of fate, of the working out of an inevitable natural process, upon which human agency could have had no impact. The eastern tribes had undoubtedly dwindled and were still diminishing, but there is no evidence that Ludlow, Logan, or M' Doal considered themselves history's losers, or the victims of an uncontrollable or irresistible dispossession.[4]

In the fall of 1823, these men and their people were actively shaping their own destiny in Indiana, particularly in the parts of the state from Madison County northward. Statehood came to Indiana in 1816, and with it a surge in the number of white settlers. In 1820 the census tallied just under 150,000 residents. This was a respectable population, but the number alone gives a misleading sense of the degree to which the state was actually settled. Eighty percent of the enumerated residents lived south of the old National Road, in the hills and river valleys of the state's southern third, an area that had received steady migration down the Ohio River and from the highlands of Tennessee and Kentucky.[5] Corydon, a village in Harrison County along the Ohio River, was still the seat of government, reflecting the demographic preponderance of Indiana's southern fringe.

Identifying the Victims

Central regions of Indiana such as Madison County, which was not formally organized and incorporated until November 10, 1823, the same month that Logan's people arrived, had only been open to white settlement for five years. Before the signing of the Treaty of Saint Marys late in 1818, this was land legally reserved to two tribes: the Miami, who had inhabited the region for some centuries, and the Delaware, who migrated into Miami land from the Susquehanna valley decades earlier, fleeing pressure from encroaching white and Iroquois populations. The center of the region's Delaware population was located in the lands drained by the White River.

The treaty settled an annuity of $4,000 per annum on the tribes, who agreed to remove west of the Mississippi River.[6] This so-called New Purchase opened millions of acres, roughly one-third of the state, to unimpeded white settlement, causing a modest land rush. The first white settler of what would become Madison County was John Rogers, an Irishman who resettled from North Carolina in December 1818, with the ink still drying on the treaty. He was followed closely by Frederick Bronnenberg, a German emigrant, and within a few years this initial trickle turned into a flood.[7] By 1823 the state was certainly in rapid transition and would more than double its total population by the time of the 1830 census. Nonetheless, the lands around Fall Creek, when Logan arrived in November 1823, were still very much the frontier.

The use of the term "frontier" has been the subject of some historical controversy. It may be understood here not as a simple line, but as a zone in which Indian and white met, mingled, contested for resources and control, and exerted cultural influence upon one another. If the frontier period is considered to be at an end when one side exercised decisive control over the other, that period in Indiana was only just arriving in the fall of 1823.[8] Only two years earlier, in September 1821, a handful of white settlers had watched the Delaware depart down the White River in twenty government-built canoes, the last formal removal of the Indians in what became Madison County.[9]

Even then, a significant Indian presence persisted. The Big Reserve, which remained in the hands of the Miami for twenty years after the Treaty of Saint Marys, stretched down into Boone Township, near the present-day town of Elwood in the far northwestern corner of Madison County.[10] Some Delaware villages remained in the area, as did villages of the Eel River Miami, and as late as 1825 small bands of Indians were reported in eastern and central Indiana.[11] The Census Bureau had its own definition of "frontier" at the time—any place where whites numbered fewer than two per square mile. By this definition, Indiana as a whole in 1820—with 147,000 people inhabiting 33,000 square miles—was not frontier. Madison County in 1823, on the other hand, with 600 whites scattered over 450 square miles, was.[12]

For the area's tribal peoples, the presence of the rapidly expanding white settlement in the vicinity of still unclaimed forests fostered a hybrid style of

A native woman pounds grain with a hominy pounder in a small hunting camp.

life, one that perpetuated ancient patterns while exhibiting a growing European influence. The ongoing fragmentation of their lands into European-style private holdings increasingly restricted the opportunities for Native Americans to fish, trap, hunt, and gather as they had done for centuries. In the mid-1820s, though, the native peoples were not yet entirely alienated from their land. Semimigratory subsistence, alternating settled agriculture with hunting and gathering, was still a viable lifestyle.

Thus a scattering of compact Indian bands such as those who became the victims at Fall Creek split their time between farm villages and isolated hunting camps. In the spring and summer they raised corn, squash, potatoes, and other crops. In the fall and winter they followed circuitous migration routes to pursue the region's abundant game, to catch fish, and to gather furs and forest products. Indiana's growing network of development and enterprise was still in its infancy, so small groups of Indians often slipped through the loose seams of European-American settlement undetected by the whites around them.

Logan and his band were living in Madison County for weeks, many sources report, before word of their presence near Big Lick spread through the white community.[13] Their skill at secluding their lives from the whites accounts partly for the fact that so little is known about them. Neither the names nor the numbers of the adult men at the Indian camp, for example, were ever established with certainty in the historical record. The only witness whose testimony survives at length is that of James Hudson, whose supposed "confession" to journalist Samuel Woodworth appears to have been thoroughly dramatized, and probably sensationalized, for publication. Hudson recalls three Indian men, whom he names Logan, the chief, and his companions Ludlow and M' Doal.[14]

Other accounts differ, even those by active participants in the trials. Oliver H. Smith, a young attorney and future U.S. senator, assisted in the prosecution of three of the killers. The memoirs he set down decades later are one of the most widely cited sources for the history of these events, and they are at times wildly inconsistent with other accounts. Smith recalled only two Indian men rather than three, and he did not even get the names of those two correct. In Smith's account, "The principal Indian was called Ludlow, and was said to be named for Stephen Ludlow, of Lawrenceburgh. The other man I call Mingo."[15]

The man referred to by Smith as Mingo, whom he describes as one of the victims of the killings near the Big Lick, can only have been Logan, whose proper name actually appears in the surviving copy of the grand jury's murder indictment against Hudson. M' Doal's name appears neither in Smith's memoir nor in most official county histories, which describe the band as led by not three but two men, of whom only Ludlow's name is recorded.[16] John Johnston, a regional agent for the Bureau of Indian Affairs stationed at Piqua, Ohio, records no names at all in his published memoirs but recalled the party in its entirety as consisting of only nine, rather than ten.[17] Sandford C. Cox, a famed Wabash valley memoirist who as a youth saw the manacled and broken Hudson with the other killers, also remembered a party of only nine.

Taken in their entirety, the conflicting reports about the size of Logan's band constitute a serious obstacle to the quest for historical accuracy. They embody rock-solid certainty itself, however, when compared with the evidence regarding the tribal identity of the murdered Indians. Surviving court documents and letters from principals in the case offer no clue, referring to the victims only as "Indians."[18] Even in the very earliest published histories, the tribal backgrounds assigned to the victims vary widely. Some describe them as a band of Shawnee and Miami; some say Miami and Seneca; others say only Delaware, or only Seneca, or "half-breed."[19] Johnston, probably the most knowledgeable source close to the case, identified them as a band of Seneca who had migrated for the winter from their homes near Lewis Town, Ohio, under the leadership of Logan.

Johnston's apparent certitude about the Seneca identity of the victims is qualified, however, by the fact that he later described one of the women as being not Seneca at all, but "Delaware, half white, and spoke English."[20] Hudson, another party obviously very close to the event, described Ludlow in his *Confession* as a half-breed. Popular tradition in Madison County helped cloud the matter, insisting for the next half century at least that Logan's wife herself was not an Indian at all, but "a white woman, possessed of much intelligence and some education."[21]

Some of the inconsistent testimony may be sorted out. As to the size and composition of the band, there can be little question that it consisted of three men, three women, and four children, regardless of those later sources that recall only two men. Traveling together in multifamily "clans" was a common practice among the Miami and other tribes of the area, such as the Potawatomi.[22] Polygamy, on the other hand, while an accepted practice, was not especially common. The most plausible case is that the three women mentioned in every account were the wives of the three men mentioned in most, especially the earliest reports, rather than the consorts of just two men.

There would have been no reason, furthermore, for sources such as Hudson to invent a male survivor if he did not exist, nor to go to the trouble of providing a name for an invented figure. It is not surprising that the escaped M' Doal, if he did in fact survive, faded from the memories of some who later recalled the incident. His fate never figured prominently either in the initial reports of the murders or in the subsequent judicial proceedings.

The precise racial and tribal backgrounds of the members of the group, in contrast, will always remain a mystery. The earliest reasonably reliable testimony is that of Johnston, who in the wake of the murders had to deal with the relatives of some of the dead Indians. Logan, as Johnston recorded, was undoubtedly from the village of Lewis Town, a settlement of mixed Shawnee and Seneca, located in the west-central Ohio county of Logan (named, in fact, for a relative of this Logan).[23] Presumably, a significant part of the band with which he traveled was drawn from this mixed Shawnee-Seneca background.

It is possible, however, that Delaware and Miami, both of whom were still present in some numbers in the county and the region, were represented in the group, as many sources later maintained. Whites captured by the Indians of the Ohio River valley had noted for decades that members of these tribes frequently intermarried, shared villages, and traveled together.[24] Missionaries, traders, and federal Indian agents also observed that Delaware, Shawnee, and Miami cohabited a number of substantial farming villages in northeastern Indiana, near the portage of the Wabash and Maumee rivers.[25] This was somewhat north of Lewis Town, but would not have been far off the migration route that Logan and his band likely followed.

By this time in the early nineteenth century, such tribally mixed groups were common throughout the Old Northwest. As Indian nations such as the Delaware declined in numbers while being forced into new lands, intertribal marriages were increasingly inviting and sensible, for a number of reasons. Necessity, of course, was partially at work. With numbers dwindling, the survival of some bands depended on finding marriage partners of childbearing age outside the group. But exogamous marriage was probably a natural development that offered other advantages to a besieged culture experiencing the upheaval that white expansion was imposing on Native Americans. Such marriages undoubtedly helped to defuse the threat of destructive interethnic violence.

The gradual emergence of a pantribal identity also promised greater chances of cultural survival when faced with the threat of an encroaching society that was not inclined to distinguish among its subject peoples.[26] The rise of the Shawnee Prophet, Tenskwatawa, in northern Indiana had successfully propagated a new native religion predicated upon just this concept of inter-tribal unity prior to the War of 1812. His most fervent and militant converts had been found among the Delaware towns along the White River, where the Prophet and his brother, Tecumseh, found refuge after the Treaty of Green-ville.[27] So the description of Logan's band as of mixed tribal background seems not only plausible but also very likely.

The same cannot be said of the identification of Logan's wife as white. This belief circulated popularly in the county and was recorded in a local newspaper article written fifty years after the massacre. Although Logan was an Indian of high status and had lived surrounded by white communities in Ohio for much of his life, such a marriage would have been unusual. The presence of a white,

IMAGES: INDIANA HISTORICAL SOCIETY

The Prophet (Tenskwatawa) was the spiritual leader of the pantribal confederacy at Prophetstown (near present-day Lafayette).

Tecumseh's confederation was the last Native American resistance movement in the Old Northwest, it was destroyed when Tecumseh was killed in the Battle of the Thames in 1813.

Christian woman at the camp, and her brutal murder, furthermore, would almost certainly have prompted some comment among the accounts generated at the time.

Johnston's assertions that one of the women was of mixed race, on the other hand, and the identification of Ludlow as a half-breed, share a high degree of historical plausibility. Mixed bloods, typically the product of a white father and Indian mother, were not unusual in the tribes of the region. They often enjoyed a high status, as would befit the wife of a chief such as Logan, due to their acculturation with whites and their greater likelihood of possessing some English-language skills.[28] And a strong implied case can also be made that Ludlow was, as Hudson alleges, the product of an interracial union. He clearly had a serviceable command of English, he is cited as having been named for a white settler, and his behavior as it appears in the recorded accounts suggests that, of all the members of the Indian group, Ludlow was the least intimidated by the whites and most at ease in their presence.

Harvesting the Wilderness: Life at the Winter Camp

While some frustrating ambiguity still surrounds the identity of Logan's band, what they were doing in the woods near the Big Lick is far more certain. Despite the absence of written accounts by the Indians themselves, the folkways of migratory native bands have been reliably and carefully reconstructed from the accounts of white captives and neighbors, especially missionaries, as well as from subsequent archaeological and anthropological research.

The horticultural skill of the Great Lakes Indian tribes is well known, and their proficiency as farmers requires little elaboration. In May or June the women of the Miami, Delaware, Seneca, and other woodland tribes planted melons, pumpkins, squash, beans, cucumbers, potatoes, and, of course, corn. The Miami in particular were known for their possession of a soft white corn that was considered more palatable than the flint corn of most of their neighbors, and per-acre yields must have been quite respectable. Early settlers testified that the Miami farming economy supported large towns whose inhabitants sometimes numbered in the thousands.[29] A dried portion of the corn surplus, furthermore, was an important subsistence staple in their travels, hence the presence of the hominy pounder at Logan's camp.

The setting for the destruction of Logan's clan, however, was strikingly different from that of the thriving Indian agricultural villages. The members of many of the woodland tribes customarily passed a third or more of each year away from their fields and villages, taking up residence in temporary hunting and sugaring camps, where they reaped a surprisingly varied bounty of goods from the forest. Every October, after taking in the last of the fall harvest, small bands scattered into the surrounding woodland, often traveling many days before settling on a campsite. Delaware, according to the evidence of missionaries, traveled up to one hundred miles from their homes to establish their camps.[30] An overland trip of this distance with children and goods must have taken four to five days travel at a minimum, barring intermediary stops for hunting. Logan's clan had traveled about one hundred miles nearly due west from their home at Lewis Town to the site of their camp on the banks of Deer Lick Creek.

Site selection was crucial, and, although not evident at first glance, the location chosen by Logan's clan along the banks of Deer Lick Creek was ideal in several respects. The area, low lying and prone to flooding after any significant precipitation, was just the sort of place avoided by the hill-dwelling early white settlers of southern Indiana. For generations after, locals referred to this mucky but fertile stretch of bottomland northeast of the early town of Pendleton as the "Prairie Swamp." But the topography also exhibits enough roll to offer numerous elevated and well-drained sites.[31]

Game roamed here in abundance, drawn by the mineral deposits at the Big Lick and by the relative scarcity of human settlement. Firewood, which the Indians consumed in large quantities, was to be had easily on every hand. The native shagbark hickory, highly valued as fuel for its hot, clean flame, flourished in the region's moist soil. The area offered—as it still does—substantial concentrated stands of the sugar maple (*Acer saccharum*), whose rendered sap was valued for both consumption and trade.

In addition, there were enough, but not too many, white people. The county was still sufficiently rugged and isolated to deter, to this point, all but an unusually hardy band of settlers, but it was also just a few miles south of the overland peddler and trading route known as the "Strawtown Trace." Following old Indian trails, the Strawtown Trace provided a pathway from Greenville, Ohio, to Chicago. The proximity of this route offered fairly reliable access to the trade goods upon which bands such as Logan's depended by the 1820s, and for which they exchanged their furs and other products.[32] At the same time, a few miles south of the Big Lick, white traders such as William and John

Conner, who played a significant role in the judicial proceedings surrounding the murders, operated thriving trading posts that were only too happy to barter whiskey or goods for the furs gathered by the Indians.

Once the choice of a site was made, the provision of shelter was the most pressing need. Contemporary accounts provide no details of the Indian dwellings, beyond describing their camp as a collection of wigwams. White observers sometimes used this term in an imprecise way, and in this case it might have referred to a number of kinds of structures constructed by the Indians (usually built by the women of the group) at their migrant locations. The true *wikiami* of the Miami was typically a compact, dome-shaped lodge, fashioned from bent saplings framed around an oval floor and covered with bark or woven mats. With a fire pit in the center vented by a central roof opening, sleeping platforms on the sides and space for storage at the rear, these snug dwellings could be built in a few hours.[33]

Travelers, missionaries, and captives among the tribes of the Ohio River valley at about this time, however, also described other sorts of Indian shelter commonly constructed for use both at permanent settlements and as bases during the wintertime hunting and sugaring seasons. On the Ohio River near Cincinnati in 1792, a party of Shawnee captured eleven-year-old Oliver Spencer, who later became a Methodist minister. He spent seven months in captivity, and in his subsequent narrative of the experience he left detailed descriptions of a gabled style of lodge in use by his captors. These were framed with hickory and elm logs, walled with broad, flattened strips of elm bark, and lined inside with more bark or deerskins. With dimensions of approximately fourteen feet by twenty-eight feet, as Spencer later recalled, these Shawnee shelters were sometimes much larger than the homes constructed by contemporary white pioneers.[34] Cox, for example, recalled that when his family first arrived in Indiana in the 1820s, they accommodated two adults and five children in a cabin measuring twelve feet by sixteen feet.[35]

Another Methodist minister, J. B. Finley, went to proselytize among the Wyandotte and other tribes of Ohio in October 1821. Finley's mission was near Sandusky, a few days distance from Fall Creek. He spent most of the next decade among the local tribes, and the memoirs he published shortly before his death in 1856 give a vivid representation of the customs of the Miami, Wyandotte, Shawnee, and others. Finley lived in a winter hunting camp at nearly the same time Logan's clan settled in at the Big Lick, in March of 1822

The Miami, Shawnee, and Winnebago men in these drawings depict the variety of clothing styles and weapons used by Native Americans in the 1820s.

or 1823, and he provides a glowing account of the conditions in such a settlement:

> Their winter hunting camps are much more comfortable, and the scenery much more pleasant, than those who have never seen them would imagine. They are built of poles, closely laid together, by cutting a notch in the upper part of the pole, and so laying the next one into it, and then stopping all the cracks with moss from the old logs. They are covered with bark, a hole being left in the middle of the roof for the smoke to go out of. The fire is in the center, and the beds are round three sides. These are raised from the earth by laying short chunks of wood on the ground, and covering them with bark laid lengthwise. On the bark is spread skins of some kind, and these are covered with blankets. The beds are three feet wide, and serve also for seats. These camps are always pitched in rich bottoms, where the pasture is fine for horses, and water convenient.[36]

The taking of game was the primary subsistence activity at these camps, and this was done both by hunting and by extensive trapping. Deer and bear were hunted for meat and skins alike and were apparently taken whenever encountered. The records of white observers suggest that the Indians were most interested in this large game in the fall, however, when the beasts were fat and plentiful and the deer hides had the hue and suppleness most desirable in trade.[37] Before the introduction of European firearms, and into the early nineteenth century, the Indians relied on simple bows made from a variety of flexible woods—mulberry, cedar, and, especially ash—and they used these according to much testimony with superlative skill. Despite the technical limitations imposed by the simple design of their bows, remarked early Indiana outdoorsman Maurice Thompson, "the fact remains that American savages were, all things considered, marvelous archers."[38]

Giving them an added advantage over their quarry was their extraordinary skill at tracking. "They were, moreover, incomparably sly, cunning, light-footed, and resourceful in pursuit of game. . . . And so light was the fall of their moccasin-shod feet, so sly their slipping between the tufts of underbrush, so great their knack of keeping always under cover of tree, or grass, or foliage, that even the most watchful bird or beast would be approached unawares," noted Thompson.[39] As the account of Ludlow's firing at the duck suggests, rifles of European or American make were increasingly supplanting these traditional weapons by the 1820s. It is also clear, however, that both Ludlow and Logan retained traditional weapons such as the tomahawk, and it is likely that they were as accustomed to the use of their traditional bow as to the use of the rifle.

The Indians took large game throughout the winter when the opportunity arose and would rouse hibernating bears when detected in hollow trees, shallow caves, and other sheltered locations. After the passing of the new year, however, the hunt for the increasingly scarce large game animals was supplanted for the remainder of the winter and spring by the taking of small animals in traps. By reason of its abundance, the raccoon was undoubtedly the most important game animal taken by trapping in the Indiana woods, though it was far from the only one.

The range covered by a small group of trapping Indians such as Ludlow, M' Doal, and Logan was enormous and must have been part of the reason for the dispersal of the community in small, scattered groups in the pursuit of the game. "One man will have, perhaps, three hundred raccoon traps, scattered over a country ten miles in extent," Finley remembered. "These traps are 'dead falls,' made of saplings, and set over a log which lies across some branch or creek, or that is by the edge of some pond or marshy place."[40] The raccoon harvest became particularly abundant in February and March, when the animals were easily caught along the waterways as they hunted the frogs emerging from ponds and creek beds. The take for a skilled trapper could be astonishing: "I have known a hunter to take from his traps thirty raccoons in two days, and sometimes they take more," Finley wrote. A good harvest for an entire season at the time would be "from three to six hundred."[41]

The raccoon, skinned, gutted, boiled whole, and eaten from the kettle, was an important staple in the winter camp, but the actual extent of the culling of small game each early spring, for meat but especially for furs to use in trade, went far beyond raccoon. The fur trade in Indiana, judged both in terms of volume and especially of value produced, peaked after the War of 1812, between about 1815 and 1830, and an analysis of records in the trade has disclosed an amazing variety of animals taken for their pelts. These included the well known, such as deer, raccoon, mink, otter, and beaver (though this was becoming rare in Indiana by the 1820s), as well as bear, muskrat, opossum, wolf, wildcat, fox of several kinds, groundhog, and even skunk.[42]

The last portion of the winter camp season was taken up with sugaring, one of the most valuable and labor intensive of the woodland Indians' subsistence activities. As the winter turned to spring and daytime high temperatures of forty degrees or so alternated with nighttime lows below the freezing point, the sap in the maples began to rise in response to subterranean seasonal warming. In a typical season around the southern Great Lakes, this point was reached in the first weeks of February, and collection of sap and its reduction by boiling continued until the sap began to lose its clarity and delicate flavor, usually sometime in the latter portion of March.

The work was arduous. The Indians gathered the sap by gouging the bark of the maples a few feet above the ground and collecting the liquid in birch-bark troughs, or, later, wooden or metal buckets. A mature, healthy maple might yield one to three gallons of the thin, watery sap each day during the season, but almost all of this was water to be boiled or frozen off and then discarded to intensify the sugar content. The boiling went on steadily over low fires for weeks at a time, requiring constant attention and considerable amounts of ready fuel. Modern sugar gatherers require about forty gallons or so of the sap to produce a single gallon of maple syrup.[43]

This extraordinarily labor intensive, but profitable, operation was primarily the work of women and children, as was the case with so many other activities of economic importance to the tribes. Spencer's account of his time laboring for his captors is indicative of the attention devoted to the task:

> It was now near the close of February, when sharp, frosty nights, and days of warm sunshine, succeeding the extreme cold of winter, constituted what in early times in the west was called sugar weather. . . . Taking our large brass kettle, with several smaller ones, some corn and beans for our sustenance, our bedding, and indeed all our household furniture and utensils, excepting the hommony block, we closed our cabin door, placing the customary stick against it, crossed the Maumee below the mouth of the Auglaize, and packing our baggage on a horse, proceeded four or five miles down the river to a beautiful open woods, principally of sugar trees, intermixed with blue ash, elm and poplar. Here Cooh-coo-cheeh had for many years made her sugar, and here we found a comfortable bark shelter, with every convenience for sugar making, save kettles, which we now supplied. I here found constant employment: dusting out and setting the troughs as the old woman tapped the trees; carrying the sap, cutting wood, making fires, and occasionally attending to boiling the water at night.[44]

Spencer records that over several days' time they collected sap sufficient to produce a "hundred weight" of sugar. Since the sap itself is 98 percent water, this would have required the collection, carrying, and reduction of some thousands of gallons of liquid. The typical boiling season lasted thirty to thirty-five days.[45] If, hypothetically, two gallons of sap per day were collected, on average, from each tapped tree, a total of sixty to seventy gallons of the sap might have been gathered from each sugar maple in a season. This would mean that Spencer and his captor, Cooh-coo-cheeh, each day probably had to tap and carry sap from somewhere between fifty and seventy trees.

The result was well worth the labor. Cooled in wooden molds in its crystallized form—that was the standard product into which the sap was rendered until syrup-tight tin containers were introduced in the Civil War era—maple sugar was easily transportable in baskets and, if kept dry, remained unspoiled indefinitely. Prior to the extensive cultivation of sugar cane later in the century, it was the only sweetener, other than honey, available on the frontier, and it was highly prized for its delicate and unique flavor.

It was also a valuable, high-energy nutriment. Finley and others report that the sugar, blended with water to make a thick molasses, was an important part of the diet of the Indians and that they used it as a complement to meat such as raccoon. Much incidental evidence suggests that the sugar was considered highly valuable in the Fall Creek area at the time of the killings. Many pioneer families—including the Sawyers—imitated the Indian techniques and maintained permanent sugaring camps in the woods. And the commodity value of the easily exchanged product made it very attractive. Ludlow, it has been noted, had quarreled violently with Phebe Hudson in an attempt to persuade her to part with some maple sugar that he allegedly planned to trade for liquor.

Nor did the bounty derived from the forests by native ingenuity end with the sugaring in late winter. Foraging while the men pursued game, the women and children of camps such as Logan's customarily added a variety of other foods to the Indian diet and contributed products to the pool of goods used in exchange with whites. They gathered honey and dug wild potatoes in March. Nuts were collected in late fall or early winter. Hemp for use in mats, baskets, and rope was gathered and worked in the winter. Fish, too, were both speared and trapped in the nearby waters. Skillful use of these "wilderness" resources prior to the arrival of the whites had provided the Indians, without inordinate labor, a plentiful sustenance.

By the time Madison County was established in 1823, though, the natural bounty of the forests no longer sufficed to meet the needs of Logan and his people. For three centuries, since the introduction of metal tools and other

European products, Indians had grown more reliant upon these goods. The dependency was so great by the time of Logan's arrival in Madison County that most of the subsistence activity of the men—taking furs and deer hides—was directed not toward immediate use or consumption by the Indians, but toward securing valuable products to trade with the whites for goods. For the Indians, the terms of exchange had become destructive by the 1820s in Madison County, as knowledgeable observers such as Lewis Cass noted.[46]

As long as the destruction of the game was restricted to an adequate supply of the wants of the Indians themselves, it is probable there was little diminution in the number of animals, and that here, as in other cases, population and subsistence had preserved an equal ratio to each other. But when the white man arrived, with his cloths, guns, and other tempting articles, and the introduction of new wants drove the Indians to greater exertions to supply them, animals were killed for their furs and skins.[47]

The enormous harvest of raccoons and other fur-bearing mammals, with demand and prices peaking in the mid-1830s, had grown far beyond the natural population's ability to sustain such losses on a yearly basis.[48]

Successive white governments in the region—French, British, American—naturally worked to foster the Indian hunger for white goods, adopting policies such as the "Civilization Act" of 1819, which encouraged the distribution of European-style agricultural implements among the tribes.[49] Ultimately, some whites hoped not only to derive personal profit from such trade, but also to so impoverish the Indians that they would be willing to exchange land to expunge their debt. One of the most notorious expressions of this strategy, if the policy may be so dignified, was conveyed by Thomas Jefferson, who urged William Henry Harrison as governor of the Indiana Territory to expand the Indian trade "and be glad to see the good and influential individuals among them run in debt, because we observe that when these debts get beyond what the individuals can pay, they become willing to lop them off by a cession of lands."[50] Federal Indian agents in Indiana, particularly John Tipton, worked hard to accommodate their superiors by fostering indebtedness among their Indian clients.[51]

The impact of new tools, weapons, and products on native culture was enormous, and the astonishing variety of goods produced for and exchanged with the Indians in the fur trade was comprehensive. Merely a partial list of the items in an inventory of the American Fur Company from 1827, for example, gives a sense of the range of needs the trade now met for the Indians: playing cards, rings, hoes, tin cups, tomahawks, wampum belts, chocolate, pepper, tea, cloves, peppermint, nutmeg, sewing thread of many colors, needles, saddles and bridles, arm and wrist bands, rifles, salt, kettles, tobacco, jew's-harps, buttons, ribbon, scissors, seeds, scythes, nails, combs, foodstuffs of many kinds, and much, much more.[52] Also included in the inventory was whiskey.

It may be, as some scholars have suggested, that the horrific impact of strong drink on the Indians, and of their propensity to insensate drunkenness, was exaggerated by white observers. We have seen, for example, that Logan refused the whiskey he was offered by the whites on the morning of his death, according to Hudson's confession. But there is ample testimony to the corrosive effect that the consumption of alcohol had on many of the Indians, which was attested to by nearly all whites who had regular contact with them, and which was the constantly lamented bane of the white missionaries who tried to convert and serve the native peoples.[53]

"No one who has not seen an Indian drunk can possibly have any conception of it," the Moravian missionary John Peter Kluge wrote. "It is as if they had all been changed into evil spirits."[54] For many, the urge to drink was an irresistible compulsion. "Their invariable habit is, not to quit the bottle or cask while a drop of strong drink remains," Charles Johnston observed of his Shawnee captors, noting that many were incapacitated for just as long as their supply of drink persisted.[55]

The abuse of ardent spirits, both in actuality and in the reputation of the Indians for drunkenness, played an important role in the murders at Fall Creek. The whites, as shall be seen, drank heavily in the days leading up to the killings, and they probably hoped to steel their group resolve by passing around their whiskey bottles at the abandoned cabin by the Big Lick immediately before shooting Ludlow and Logan.[56] The mutilation of the Indian bodies at Logan's camp, which is likely to strike modern observers as mere gratuitous barbarity, also has links to the consumption of alcohol, both as practiced by the whites that morning, in whom it probably served to loosen inhibitions against indiscriminate violence, and as a component of prevalent white beliefs about Indian practice.

The disfigurement of the corpses, to the extent it can be established to have occurred, was universally considered at the time to be an effort to make the crimes seem the result of a drunken Indian rage. And this ploy was in fact plausible in the Madison County of 1824 because Delaware Indians had in the past few years committed just such crimes upon their own families. In 1819 the Baptist missionary Isaac McCoy noted the connection between drunkenness and Indian violence: "John (a Wea companion) informed me that a few yards from where we slept, an Indian not long before had killed his wife with a knife, which was the third wife that he had murdered. About three nights previous to our departure, the brother of the same murderer, in a drunken frolic, killed two women with a tomahawk."[57]

The ubiquity of powerful distilled spirits, and their poisonous impact on the Indians and on their relations with the whites, illustrates the dangerous fragility and risk of Indian life on the fringes of the white community. Their wandering, partially concealed style of winter living permitted some remnants of the native tribes to preserve valued folkways through a transitional, quasi-traditional *modus vivendi*. But in the setting of an aggressively expanding settler society, this way of life was chancy. Some of the material products of the surrounding white society, especially tools, weapons, and alcohol, may have presented an irresistible attraction. Embracing these things meant accepting a connection to a world that was incompatible with their cultural traditions. As time passed, this connection dissolved the stability of many of the very patterns of life that the Indians seem to have wished to preserve.[58]

Far worse, though, was the ever-present risk of deadly friction with the settlers. In immediate proximity stood two essentially separate societies, characterized by wildly divergent notions of property rights, of accepted economic practice, of law, and of family structure. Sometimes, perhaps more often than is generally recognized, both sides found the prospect of coexistence an inviting one. Just as often, though, the opposite was the case. As the white society multiplied its numbers and penetrated Indian lands, malignant intercultural tensions poisoned attitudes between the two increasingly unequal groups. The barest pretexts, under these conditions, often sufficed to precipitate the most extreme violence.

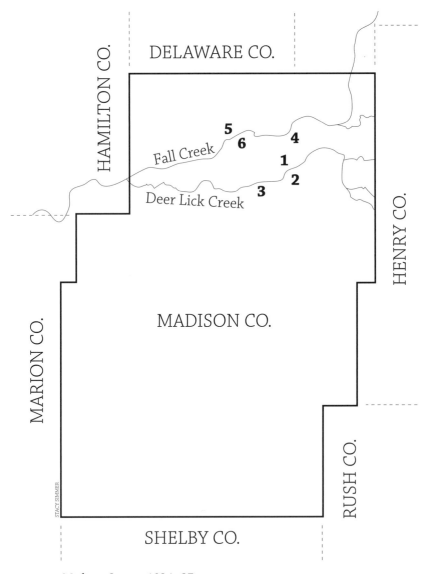

HAMILTON CO.

DELAWARE CO.

HENRY CO.

MARION CO.

MADISON CO.

RUSH CO.

SHELBY CO.

Fall Creek

Deer Lick Creek

5
6
4
1
2
3

STACY SIMMER

Madison County, 1824–27
1. *The site of Logan's camp*
2. *The site of the "hog wallow" where the bodies were dumped*
3. *The site of the "Big Lick" where Logan was killed*
4. *The site of the Sawyer homestead*
5. *The site of the "Prairie Swamp"*
6. *The site of the falls at Pendleton*

3

Murder in Their Hearts
Settlers and Killers in Early Madison County

"The voice of nature's very self drops low,
As though she whispered of the long ago,
When down the wandering stream the rude canoe
Of some lone trapper glided into view,
And loitered down the watery path that led
Through forest depths that only knew the tread
Of savage beasts; And wild barbarians
That skulked about with blood upon their hands
And murder in their hearts."[1]

JAMES WHITCOMB RILEY

Mass murder was difficult to conceal, even in a venue as thinly settled as Madison County in the spring of 1824. Before the day was out, local rumor hinted at something amiss in the woods. Reports of heavy gunfire, the sudden absence of the Indians, talk overheard by neighbors in the Bridge and Sawyer homes, all of these suggested mischief to the county's scattered community of settlers. The morning after the killings a party of locals assembled to investigate. They were headed by Sheriff Samuel Cory and included members of the Bridge and Jones families. They soon found the gruesome evidence of the carnage that had overtaken Logan's wigwams—naked, mutilated bodies in a heap and a campground spattered with blood and littered with bits of brain and bone.

Local settlers suspected Thomas Harper and Andrew Sawyer as soon as the crime became known, and even before any evidence specifically pointing to their guilt had come to light. The fact that these particular individuals were quickly singled out by their neighbors in a community where rowdy, physically violent behavior was commonplace, requires some explanation. Convulsive changes, compressed into a brief span of only a few years, were transforming Madison County. As new lands were wrested from Indian control, settlers in the county forged a way of life that many found rewarding. At the same time, however, the enduring legacy of frontier violence sometimes generated tensions that exploded beyond the control of the emerging white community.

The Rage of Thomas Harper

Madison County during this first decade of statehood was still a characteristically migrant society. As in other transitional zones in the Old Northwest, its newly arrived and growing white population was enterprising, aggressive, turbulent, and deeply fractured by competing communities of interest. Obviously, for their white inhabitants—the only ones for whom a legal entity such as Madison County existed at the time—these zones of new development were also magnets of opportunity. A burgeoning contingent of settled small farmers, traders, land speculators, and public officials formed this community's predominant component. They saw themselves surrounded by enormous potential material wealth. They also envisioned the region blessed by commercial and agricultural prosperity that would soon, as one put it in 1821, "convert the gloomy woods into fields waving with luxuriant harvests."[2]

Its members accordingly favored the quick establishment of the legal order, such as strict protection of property rights, and physical infrastructure—"internal improvements," in the political jargon of the day—that would ensure future prosperity. On the fringes of this community, though, was a significant population of rowdy, often lawless transients. These "ornery movers," as pioneer memoirist Sandford C. Cox termed them, were restless men in nearly constant search of greener grass along the leading edge of the frontier. They lived off the abundance of the wild lands and eked out their existence through seasonal labor and occasional crime.

Though often able to benefit from the bond of their common racial identity, these renegades led lives that brought frequent conflict with others in the region's white society. Drunken violence, thievery, and unscrupulous—hence provocative—commerce with the Indians were often attributed to such interlopers. Many settlers, wary and suspicious, kept a distance from these rootless undesirables. Nevertheless, two forces transcended class and social distinctions in the white community, binding the marginalized and itinerant frontiersman to the settled pioneer—family ties and a shared fear of the Indians.

Thomas Harper, whose arrival in central Indiana ignited the slaughter of Logan's band, was a walking embodiment of everything that threatened the tranquility and economic prospects of the settler community. Harper came to Madison County sometime in early March 1824, drawn by bonds of blood shared with the Bridge family. His sister, Mary, was married to John T. Bridge Sr. She bore him nine children in Ohio and Kentucky, before moving with the family to Indiana in 1819; she died two years later. Harper resided in Butler County, in the southwestern corner of Ohio, before arriving in Madison County that rainy spring for a visit with his brother-in-law, nieces, and nephews.[3] Described as a restless and roving frontiersman, of uncertain age, but apparently fit and relatively young, the landless, unmarried, hard-drinking Harper was a loose cannon—an itinerant integrated into the white community with only the loosest ties.[4]

He was also a white man seething with rage. Harper's barely controlled anger, perhaps a result of his impoverished and rootless condition, permeates contemporary portrayals of him. Whatever its source, all his venom expressed itself in an intense hatred focused upon one target—the Indian. James Hudson later recalled Harper telling him, days before the murders, that "all Indians ought to be killed." Others alleged that Harper liked to boast of the number of Indians he had killed, declaring that "it was no worse to kill an Indian than a deer."[5] Although apocryphal, the story of Harper's comparison of killing Indians to hunting wild game conveys some idea of the intensity of the Indian-hating aura he emanated.

Even in a society where prejudice against the natives was ubiquitous, Harper's ferocious racial antipathy struck many of his peers as something unusual. While his hatred may have drawn nourishment from many sources, Harper's family background in southern Ohio undoubtedly played an important part in shaping his attitudes. Indian warriors terrorized the white populations of Hamilton and Butler counties in the years before the Battle of Fallen Timbers in 1794, burning villages and exterminating isolated farm families. Although Harper's father, William, arrived with his family in Butler County a few years after this, in 1798, memories remained vivid.

A decade before Harper's visit to Madison County, early in the War of 1812, resurgent Indian raiding parties once again loosed a reign of terror across the region, launching sudden hit-and-run raids to burn farms, slaughter pioneer families, and abduct captives. White farmers died both in southern Ohio and just over the border in the far southern Indiana Territory, where, in September 1812, a Shawnee raiding party systematically butchered twenty-four whites, many of them children, at the Pigeon Roost Massacre.[6]

These episodes were branded into the memories of the settler community, with the raids of the 1812 conflict leaving a particularly long-lasting and bitter legacy among the region's whites.[7] There is reason to believe that Harper experienced the impact of such violence very directly. A history of Butler County declares that several members of the Harper family—Thomas had sisters and three brothers, James, Joseph, and John—had "been massacred by the Indians" some years before the events at Fall Creek.[8] Harper himself later alluded to a brother killed by the Indians, which some sources suggest occurred at the infamous massacre of captured and defenseless American soldiers on the Raisin River during the War of 1812.

Nor did this exhaust the list of Harper's personal grievances against the Indians. Another family member, his youngest sister, Elizabeth, was kidnapped as a three-year-old in the spring of 1800, disappearing into Indian society for more than forty years. The beloved child's disappearance devastated Harper's family. Her distraught parents exhausted themselves in desperate efforts at recovery, making arduous and futile overland trips to Indian encampments as distant as Cleveland and Detroit, and, according to local lore, eventually dying of their exertions.[9] As Harper must have seen it, there could be no forgiveness for the enormity of Indian crimes.

The Harper family nursed its wrath, and Thomas carried his hatred with him, like a contagious and virulent disease, to Madison County. His visit to his Bridge relatives in that spring of 1824 may also have intensified a sense of bitterness, giving the unattached itinerant a glimpse into a way of community living from which he must have felt somewhat isolated. It is true that Harper appears to have been related by blood and by marriage to many in Madison County's small white community. There was his brother-in-law, Bridge Sr., with his brood of young sons and daughters.[10] He also appears to have been related to Andrew Sawyer, a connection mentioned in many early sources, but in unclear ways. According to some, Sawyer was also a brother-in-law of Harper by marriage to another of Harper's sisters. Others suggest that Bridge, Harper's brother-in-law, had remarried one of Sawyer's family. In either case, Harper was able to claim ties to a number of families in southern Madison County. In the Bridge and Sawyer families, however, the unattached Harper found windows into a way of life strikingly different from his own.

Kidnapping was a common practice among tribal bands on the frontier. Frances Slocum was taken from her family in Pennsylvania when she was five years old. Her family never gave up the search for her. When they finally found her she was a grown woman who had married a Miami chief and was living near present-day Peru.

Peril, Hardship, and Comfort: The Settler's World

The Bridge and Sawyer families had been residents in Madison County for some years and were thus well established by the standards of the day. Bridge Sr., born in Boston during the Revolutionary War, was a son of the Lexington revolutionary Samuel Bridge. He and his family settled first in Kentucky then in Hamilton County, Ohio, before removing to the future Madison County in 1819. They also were blistered by vivid memories of the savage Indian violence during the recently concluded war. Described as a lanky man habitually clothed in a brown coat, Bridge had a stooped posture and balding pate that made him look older than his forty-five years. Of Sawyer, less is known. Unlike Bridge, he does not appear in the Indiana census lists of 1820, but Cox later described him as powerfully built and swarthy. He was known to have spoken Dutch (and was thus perhaps a first- or second-generation immigrant) and was commonly seen in clothing of faded blue linsey-woolsey, the durable fabric of mixed linen and wool that was a standard homemade product on the frontier.[11]

The world inhabited by these householders and their families was in important ways far different from that of a wanderer such as Harper. Danger was abundant, and the pioneer was plagued by anxiety about deadly illnesses, failed crops, violent Indians and settlers, and crippling or fatal injury. But the characteristic tone of the frontier memoirist, be it a man such as Cox or a woman such as Lydia Bacon, is nostalgic rather than melancholy.[12] No doubt this is due in part to the natural tendency to romanticize youthful recollection.

But the stories of the Indiana frontier passed down after it vanished also convey a sense of the myriad genuine consolations that sweetened life and softened the hardship: the satisfaction of profiting from arduous but honest labor, the stately pace and reassuring rhythms of the agricultural calendar, the sense of communal interdependence, and the pioneer's aesthetic satisfaction in the natural beauty of the frontier countryside. Similar to the natives into whose domain they migrated, the settlers evolved a fulfilling way of life that was closely connected with their land.

The acquisition of legal title to such land was the shining dream that lured most of those who followed the frontier traces westward. As an observer of the migration put it in the 1830s, the new occupants flooding the western lands were farmers, and "very few of these are willing to be tenants of other men. They nearly all are, or desire to become, freeholders."[13] In the New Purchase of the 1820s, the business of converting the recently procured Indian land into sellable, legally defined parcels was booming. In pursuit of Jefferson's vision of a nation of self-reliant yeoman farmers, the federal government, which held title to all lands acquired from native peoples, took a freehanded approach to making the pioneer's freehold dream attainable.

The eagerness of the national government to transfer title of former Indian lands to settled white farmers verged upon fiscal recklessness in its generosity, creating a sudden frontier debt crisis. The Harrison Land Law of 1800 provided for the sale of federal lands at a price of not less than $2.00 per acre, in half-section units of 320 acres. Thus the would-be freeholder needed to come up with at least $640.

While this was a considerable sum that seemed at first glance to discourage the aspiring settler of modest means, thus favoring wealthy speculators over working farmers, the law provided for land sales by installment on the basis of a modest down payment. The purchaser could pay over a four-year period, putting down only the six dollar surveying fee and ten cents per acre at the time of sale. Perhaps predictably, generous credit terms quickly proved to be a disaster. Cash was scarce for the frontier farmer, who displayed a surprisingly optimistic tendency to overestimate his ability to generate funds for payment of debts. An epidemic of defaults and delinquencies on rash purchases of government land was the inevitable result.[14]

Populist congressmen worked to rescue the debt-pressed frontier farmer, but a series of amendments and a dozen relief measures before the panic of 1819 failed to remedy the Harrison law's shortcomings. In 1820 a comprehensively restructured land policy offered a less generous credit, but reduced the minimum lot size to eighty acres, at a new minimum price of $1.25 per acre. Now, for a single payment of $100, a man could establish himself on a scale to support a family. And legislators, delightfully responsive to the frontiersman's universal, healthy, and vigorous hatred of taxes, kept the burden of supporting the state very light. Besides a nominal poll tax and some trifling levies on specific types of property, the struggling settler had only to pay the tax on land, the chief generator of wealth. This was levied at a laughably light annual rate of $1.50 per hundred acres of "first-rate," $1.00 on "second-rate," and $0.75 on "third-rate."[15]

It is entirely possible that Cox, who spent an afternoon at the Crawfordsville land office in 1824, witnessed the parceling off of a good chunk of Madison County and may even unknowingly have seen some of those who would play a role in the events at Fall Creek. Most of the lands of the New Purchase were sold through two land offices, one at Crawfordsville (which before

1823 had been at Terre Haute) and one at Brookville, which was transferred to Indianapolis in 1825.[16] It was at such an auction one year earlier, on February 15, 1823, that Andrew Sawyer established himself in the county. Putting down his $100, Sawyer purchased a lot defined by the government land survey as the southwest quarter in the western one-third of section 15, in the 8th range of Madison County township 18 north. Sawyer's eighty-acre holding, at a site that is now on the north side of Indiana State Road 36, was due north of Logan's camp on Deer Creek by an almost exact distance of one mile.[17]

The pioneer was a subsistence farmer. So when Sawyer, the Bridges, and others like them selected their parcels, often "squatting" on their chosen site prior to acquiring legal title through the land office, they were pressed from the start to provide nearly all basic necessities for themselves. Shelter and food, naturally, topped the list. The woods that afforded such bounty to Indian and frontiersman alike were in one respect a great enemy. Trees had to be cleared and the land opened to sunlight before the settler family could start to cultivate its staple foods. So the pioneer and his family, newly arrived at the chosen homestead site, hurried to create some kind of cultivable clearing, typically even before constructing any permanent shelter.

With no more equipment than a simple woodsman's axe, clearing the land was a backbreaking job for the would-be farmer, requiring many years of hard labor before completion. New settlers started with a first crop of vegetables and grain in any small open patches on the lot. Then the labor of clearing began in earnest. Cutting out and burning the smaller trees and dense undergrowth comprised most of this work. Many of the giants of these virgin forests simply defied the puny efforts of the pioneer and his axe. Sycamores, tulip trees, and other poplars in the New Purchase could easily reach trunk diameters of eight to ten feet, and giants of fifteen feet in diameter were not unknown. Trees of such dimensions were not cleared but "girdled." A deep trench was hewn into the bark with an axe around the whole circumference of the tree, which over the course of the next season lost its foliage and died off. Gray, leafless skeletons, the dead trunks of these titans might stand scattered through the farmer's new fields for many years, while the ground between was annually plowed, harrowed, and planted.[18]

Grueling as the work could be, none of the settlers doubted that the clearing of the land was worth the effort. Indiana's forest soil, stripped of its trees, was fabled for its fertility, especially the acreage in the flat, well-watered till plain located in Madison County at the heart of the New Purchase. A month after the killings on Fall Creek, a pioneer newly arrived at Richmond, a few miles east of Madison County, wrote home to his Connecticut relations of the land's unbelievable richness. "I am in a country at present where the soil is sufficiently rich without the labour and expense of manuring and too rich to bear wheat when first cleared, but after the second year of cultivation it produces the finest of it," wrote young Nathan Smith.[19]

In his role as planter and plowman, the forest was the settler's enemy. In his role as home builder, it was his invaluable ally. The pioneer might make do for a season with sleeping quarters in a covered cart or wagon, or in a damp hole cut into the side of the most convenient hummock, but there was always considerable urgency to the task of getting a more comfortable and substantial dwelling in place. The virgin forests offered a plentiful supply of trees with trunks that were straight for eighteen to twenty feet, and these formed the basic building materials of the ubiquitous pioneer log cabin of the Old Northwest.

Depending on the degree of labor put into finishing the logs, the cabins went by a number of names—"scotched," "hewed," and others—but they were essentially built and constructed in the same way. A rectangle in some small open space was cleared of stumps, and some weeks might be spent in cutting, trimming, and dragging or rolling logs into four piles around this site. On the date chosen for the "raising," families gathered from miles around so that the adult males could assemble the structure. Without the use of nails, usually with no more than axes, perhaps an adze and some metal-tipped pike poles, the logs were notched at each end with a "seat" and a "saddle" to fit the logs that would be above and below. Teams of men raised the cabin walls into place. A "corner man" finished by aligning and leveling the four corners using few tools. All this was accomplished in a long morning of strenuous group effort.[20]

The finished polygon was typically a single room with walls six feet in height, enclosing a rectangle of perhaps 180 square feet, with mud and plaster stuffed into the chinks between logs. Shorter, progressively smaller logs were stacked upon each short side of the polygon to create two gables, to which the ridgepole was then fastened. Covered with split oak or ash clapboards laid over a series of roof poles, furnished perhaps with a stone chimney and a flimsy door hung on rawhide hinges, a day's labor might well complete the dwelling. Cut log ends, known as puncheons, provided flooring to keep the family's goods off the dirt.

The single room thus enclosed, often with no window openings, would serve as kitchen, parlor, bedroom, and storehouse for all the pioneer family's valuable belongings. These dwellings, the iconic symbol of the hardy, impover-

This cabin was built by the Thomas Lincoln family in 1817.

ished settler, were admittedly primitive, but nonetheless triumphs of anonymous architecture. Built of freely available material with the simplest tools, and without drawing, plan, or measurement, they were affordable, easy to maintain, proof against the extremes of the midwestern seasons, and barring fire, sturdy to the point of indestructibility.

The pioneer, like the Indian, also turned to the bounty of the forest for sustenance, especially in the first year or two of settlement. The Hoosier frontiersman with his single-shot long rifle harvested the still-plentiful deer and small game, valuing especially the succulent, flavorful flesh of the wild turkey. Nuts, berries, and wild fruits such as the persimmon and the crab apple, usually gathered by the children and women, supplemented an often bland and repetitive diet when they were in season. The pioneer sweet tooth found ample satisfaction in the maple sugar first harvested by the Indians. Many families, such as the Sawyers, emulated their native predecessors, maintaining their own sugaring camp, to which they annually retired when the sap rose at winter's end.

Gathering what the land offered so readily, the pioneer remained preeminently a farmer. And corn, then as now, was king in Indiana. The plant flourished in Indiana's soil and climate, yielding almost twice as much food per acre

A two-story double log cabin.

as grains such as rye, buckwheat, or oats, which were also widely sown. Corn
was easily stored and later consumed in a number of forms, boiled as mush,
pounded and milled into meal for bread, shelled and then boiled or fried to
make hominy, baked into cornpone, and fermented and distilled into bour-
bon whiskey. Within two decades of statehood, Indiana's harvest was yielding
more than fifty bushels annually per capita, and it ranked fourth in the nation
in production.[21] Pigs, adept at foraging in the forest undergrowth, provided
a reliable source of protein. The nearly unvarying diet of corn and pork could
become monotonous—coffee and sugar were delicacies, and even salt was
difficult to come by—but no one who was able to work starved on the Indiana
frontier.

And work they did. Mechanical devices were rare, so agricultural abundance was possible only through the intensive labor of many individuals.
Families were large—Indiana's birth rate in the 1810s and 1820s was among
the highest in the world—and everyone shared in the cultivation of the
fields.[22] Other tasks were typically apportioned by gender or age. Men trapped
and hunted game, women kept herb and vegetable gardens to vary the diet
with potatoes, squash, melons, or cabbage, and children scoured the woods
for fruit and "bee trees" that furnished wax and honey. The pioneer woman's

labor was especially important to the household's "manufacturing economy." Spinning thread from wool and flax, weaving cloth, and producing the family clothing was the work of mothers and daughters, as was most of the cooking, the creation of bedclothes, and the care of livestock and farm animals. Each day's work typically went on as long as there was light or, as the saying ran, "from kin to kaint"—see, that is.

Although a wearying existence, it did not lack compensations. Foremost among these was faith, in the form of enthusiastic, evangelical Protestantism. A handful of Jews, a few more Catholics, and a good many unchurched pioneers—far too many for some of their more censorious, observant neighbors—settled the Indiana forest and prairie. But the overwhelming bulk of the population followed the doctrines of reformed Christianity, mostly (but far from exclusively) as interpreted by the Methodist, Baptist, and Presbyterian churches.

Methodist circuit riders, following first eight and then many more circuits, to reach as many as a score of churches on each circuit, were particularly popular and effective preachers. The numbers of Methodists grew much more quickly than the general Indiana population, more than quintupling between 1826 and 1840, when they numbered more than fifty thousand in the state.[23] The great camp meetings held in a revival atmosphere were the community's most socially acceptable diversion from work, and they drew large crowds. Popular devotion could also lend a stern moralistic tone to public life. The public use of oaths, for example, already was a misdemeanor subject to fines in Indianapolis in the 1820s.

The message of the Methodist circuit rider was delivered by men who usually had no theology degree but were disposed of a vast fund of common sense, folk wisdom, and close acquaintance with scripture. It was related to the pioneer in simple, direct terms. Perhaps their message partook more of an Old Testament flavor than is entirely congenial to some modern Christians. Bridge Sr., for example, was certainly not making a reference to the Gospel message of Jesus when he reminded his faltering son that the Scripture commands us to kill our enemies. The allusion to Scripture itself, however, suggests the considerable degree to which biblical awareness and authority were woven into the lives of even the marginally literate Protestant frontiersman. And this evangelistic biblical sensibility found its most popular medium of expression in frontier Indiana not in the Sabbath observance, at a time when preachers were still sufficiently scarce that they had to be shared between congregations,

A visit from a circuit rider not only fed the pioneer community's spiritual needs but also provided an opportunity for far-flung neighbors to gather and socialize.

but in the camp meeting. Proclaiming an appealing message of God's grace, the goodness of work, and the possibility for redemption, the Methodist camp meeting might draw hundreds of fervent pioneer believers for days of prayer, preaching, and hymn singing.

Sharing the comfort of religion was only one of many opportunities to counter the isolation that could dog the lives of the widely scattered early settlers. The occasional loner aside, the pioneer woman and man appear to have been notably gregarious. No excuse to congregate with neighbors was neglected, and the social side of worship, labor, weddings, and similar occasions frequently eclipsed the ostensible reason for coming together. Sabbaths, complained ministers such as Henry Ward Beecher, became simple excuses for visiting and conversing; the pioneer was far happier with sermons that entertained rather than those that edified.[24] Cabin raisings and logrollings, sugaring, husking and harvesting, spinning, sewing and quilting, and significant laborious tasks of all kinds assumed a social function, reinforcing community solidarity among the scattered homesteaders.

Sexual selection was obviously an important part of such gatherings. Marriages were often contracted before a couple had passed their midteens, and young men and women whose courting may have been somewhat hampered in the setting of one-room log cabins were encouraged to exploit any opportune social occasion. Aside from courting, however, most pioneer amusements were segregated by gender. The men wrestled, raced horses, and held shooting contests with the rifles that they carried everywhere. Shooting from one hundred yards for whiskey, venison, or other prizes—and of course for the sake of reputation—the rifleman would try to drive a nail fixed in a tree, or strike a paper diamond six inches across. The women, meanwhile, typically pursued their socializing in the midst of shared domestic chores, such as apple paring, carpet tacking, goose plucking, or rag cutting.

Powerful drink was a crucial part of such social occasions. Although preachers occasionally inveighed against the dangers of liquor, the idea of abstinence was entirely alien to backwoods America in the 1820s. Temperance in any organized form was still at least a decade away from the Indiana frontier, and circuit riders themselves at this time were known to turn to a tot of whiskey to take the chill off a raw day. Liquor was untaxed—the attempt to impose an excise had incited a near revolution at the time of the Whiskey Rebellion (1794)—and every neighborhood had a still producing corn whiskey for sale at rates, in 1819, of twelve cents per half pint. Under these conditions, not surprisingly, drink was consumed in copious amounts.

This made a lot of sense. Much of the harvest could be easily preserved in distilled form, and whiskey was a readily marketable commodity of reliable value. Tea and coffee were virtually unavailable, and since every home had its whiskey jug a stiff toddy often accompanied dinners. And in an era without aspirin or any other cheap or easily available analgesic, the use of liquor afforded some relief to bodies aching from physical exertion and perhaps struggling against the chronic pain of infections, arthritis, rheumatism, strained backs, and pulled muscles.

Still, the omnipresent jug caused problems for the pioneers just as it did for the Indians. While no house or barn raising could go on without whiskey at hand—the volunteers would simply go home—much of the emphasis on finishing the task early in the day was in recognition of the fact that the work became dangerous as the day wore on and the laboring party went through several rounds of the jug. Injuries were commonly attributed to too much liquor at such events and, even more predictably, derangement through the use of alcohol was a key contributor to violence.

While the dangers posed by alcohol abuse were significant, they paled in comparison to the threat that disease posed to frontier families. The health of the Indiana pioneer was precarious, due to the prevalence of deadly biological pathogens, an unbalanced diet, poor hygiene, and ignorance. Mortal illness was terrifyingly tragic and commonplace, hanging like a willful and capricious Damocles sword over every frontier family. Fever preoccupies the correspondence of frontier mothers and for good reason.[25] The undrained swamps, backwaters, and matted undergrowth of the Ohio River frontier served as a cozy petrie dish for nurturing dangerous microbes. Typhoid fever, tuberculosis, milk sickness, dysentery, and especially malaria stalked backwoods Indiana during the first quarter of the nineteenth century.

Malaria, in the chronic, debilitating form of "ague" or in the various suddenly lethal forms with names such as "black water fever" and others, was especially widespread in late summer and early fall. Though most families kept a tonic of mixed whiskey and quinine on hand, it was of little use. This disease also played a part in the Hoosier settlers' preference for hill country over the more fertile lowlands. Though the mechanism of its transmission was unknown, the widespread and empirically based belief was that deadly fevers were less likely to strike in the well-drained hill country. Typhoid, especially in the vicinity of settlements where the drinking water was contaminated, was a constant threat as well. Tuberculosis, spreading through crowded and badly ventilated cabins, could wipe out entire families.

Ceaseless and exhausting labor, an unbalanced diet, and a complete absence of medicines or health care beyond folk cures left the settler community biologically fragile and vulnerable. Mortality rates, especially among infants and children, were very high, and overall average life expectancy in the 1820s may not have been much above forty years. By some estimates, as many as one in two live pioneer births may have died before reaching the age of six.[26] Nor were adults less vulnerable. Thriving communities simply vanished from unnamed plagues. By 1825, for example, the well-known boomtown of Hindostan in central Indiana's Martin County boasted a mill, a ferry near the falls of the White River, several businesses, and the county courthouse. Pestilence struck in 1827—probably malaria or yellow fever—and wiped the promising settlement off the map.[27]

The frequent absence of even the most elementary hygienic measures exacerbated this horrific situation, offering fertile breeding ground for the vectors who spread many of these diseases. Until the land was drained, mosquitoes multiplied in hordes, flies were trapped by the pint, and bedbugs and fleas teemed in dirty cabins. Water, taken unfiltered from streams and rivers in places where human waste was simply dumped, carried typhoid, dysentery, and, eventually, cholera. The mysterious milk sickness, long afterward discovered to be conveyed in the milk of cows that had consumed the white snakeroot plant, brought death after a week of increasing lethargy, painful bodily swelling, and excruciating suffering. Known as "the staggers" or "the trembles," it sometimes depopulated entire villages. Among its thousands of Hoosier victims was Nancy Hanks Lincoln, mother of young Abraham Lincoln.[28]

Disease, the great scourge of the frontier, was a menace far greater than that of human violence originating in the settler's social environment. Certainly, the frontier community could be a quarrelsome, rough-and-tumble place, where disagreements often ended in assault, litigation, or both. Popular opinion tolerated a level of physical force in everyday life far greater than that which was commonly accepted later. Many of the leading figures of early Madison County, for instance, were punished in court for scuffles that would today cause career-ending scandals. Moses Cox, county clerk and recorder, was arrested and fined after pleading guilty to assault on several occasions;

Disease was a greater killer than violence on the frontier. Milk sickness, which was caused by cows eating the white snakeroot plant, decimated families and communities.

Calvin Fletcher, one of the first lawyers admitted to the bar in the county and part of the defense team for Hudson, Sawyer, and the Bridges, was fined two dollars after admitting to beating up a rival lawyer; and Andrew Sawyer was the defendant, on a charge of slander, in the first trial ever heard in the newly formed county. Cox neglected to record the verdict, but Sawyer's accuser, Conrad (or in some sources, "Conrod") Crosley, was later one of the men who stood guard over the accused murderer.[29]

Some degree of violence and litigious bickering was therefore a given part of frontier community life. Madison County was shocked by the killings at Fall Creek, however, because deliberate, deadly violence, as opposed to spontaneous scuffles or fistfights, was not especially common on the farming frontier. Abnormally high rates of homicide plagued frontier mining communities, railroad towns, Western ranches, and other venues packed with single young men and few women or families, giving rise to the later popular image of the frontier as the scene of indiscriminate bloodletting. The gender imbalance typical of the most violent frontier settings, however, was not an issue for the Hoosier pioneer. The settler of the Old Northwest was typically a family man, moving westward with the company and essential support of wife and children. He was not a very likely killer, and the incomplete statistical evidence that is available suggests that murder rates in rural midwestern counties were probably quite low.[30] Only the right influences were needed, however, to trigger the placid frontiersman's potential inclination to violence.

The Road to Mass Murder

From a distance of nearly two centuries, it is practically impossible to trace the activities of Harper and his accomplices in the days before the carnage at Logan's camp with any certainty. The surviving sources are few, and they generally address the events that led up to the killings only incidentally. All the accounts, furthermore, are written by whites, although they embody a number of perspectives on the events at Fall Creek. The brief pamphlet relating the confession of Hudson provides some tantalizing details about the relations of local white men with Logan and Ludlow. One of the great-grandchildren of Bridge Sr., a woman named Helen Thurman, published a short account of the affair from her family's perspective a century after the events. One or two contemporary newspaper articles, which were naturally more concerned with giving readers the gory details of the killings than with discussing the motives of the murderers, also remain. As a body of historical testimony, this is both slim and dubious. Some important insights may be gleaned from even this paltry fund of documents, however, and to a certain extent these sources permit a cautious reconstruction of events in the days before the killings.

One fact is clear: dangerous tensions between parts of the white and Indian communities along Fall Creek were brewing for weeks before the killings. Indeed, relations were so bad that at least one attempt was made to murder the Indians with poison before the slaughter erupted at Logan's camp. The insistence on the peaceful and inoffensive behavior of the Indians found in so many later sources suggests that an awareness of these tensions did not extend through the entire white community. Or it may be that the conventional view of the Indians coexisting amicably with the white community derives from a wish to distance the killers from that community, by making their behavior seem even more outrageously exceptional than it was.

The evidence suggests that whatever its origins, this tradition of benign coexistence tells only a part of the story and tells it in a way that has given rise to serious historical confusion. The failure to appreciate the intensity of the growing friction between whites and Indians obscures historical understanding of the murders to this day. The acts of the white killers are customarily seen in one of two ways, either as the outcome of the banditry of the covetous Harper, or as a mere outburst of spontaneous racist violence—inspired by the devil, as the court documents insisted, or by the twisted character of Harper, as local tradition affirms.

An account in the local newspaper on the fiftieth anniversary of the murders is typically inattentive to motive, saying only that Harper appeared (from Kentucky rather than Ohio), and a few weeks thereafter he "persuaded his relatives that the Indians ought to be killed."[31] An early history of the town of Pendleton echoes the same theme, expressing surprise at Harper's supposed ability to manipulate his accomplices into carrying out the killings. "Harper conceived the idea of gaining possession of the property belonging to the Indians," the author declares. "He carefully planned the murder and then approached his neighbors upon the subject. Strange as it may appear, he found it an easy task to persuade them to enter into the plot."[32]

A careful consideration of the available sources suggests that the motivation for the killings was more complex than either theft or racism, and that, rather than being strange, Harper's design actually seemed logical and justifiable to many in the white community. Thievish intent and the generalized racial hatred of some whites obviously played an important role in the killings, but the demise of Logan's band was the result of neither of these. Instead, the Indians at the sugar camp were butchered as a response to specific conflicts between individuals. For reasons that were not illogical, the white killers believed that the Indians at Deer Lick Creek were a threat to their persons and property. Harper the Indian-hater was able to "persuade" his friends and relatives because growing ill will between them and the Indians made violence seem like a rational response to dangerous hostility. This hostility was most clearly expressed in the conflict between three young white men—Hudson, Harper, and Bridge—and one young Indian—Ludlow.

Hudson, a native of Baltimore, Maryland, had moved with his family to Kentucky in 1801, at the age of four. Later, he went on to Ohio and Indiana. Although he makes no allusion to previous Indian troubles in his subsequent confession, local traditions recorded in several sources say that he, like Harper, had lost relatives in Indian attacks. And in 1811, Indians either murdered or kidnapped every member of a numerous family of Hudsons who were homesteading on the Wabash River, with only the head of the family escaping. Allegedly, the Indians boiled alive the newborn baby of this Hudson family. It is not clear that these victims were in fact the relatives of James Hudson, but some evidence points toward the possibility, and it would certainly make Hudson's willingness to inflict violence on Logan's group less strange and inexplicable.[33]

Such speculation aside, there is incontestable evidence of ample cause for Hudson's hostility to the Indians out at the winter camp. Reference has already been made to Hudson's allegation that Ludlow had threatened his wife. Although freely confessing his guilt, and claiming to repent of his deeds, Hudson attributes several threatening acts to Ludlow over the course of what seems to be seven to ten days before the murders. The first such incident occurred several days prior to the killings, when Hudson stumbled unknowingly upon the Indian camp while hunting a missing cow. He relates that after some conversation, Ludlow, a half breed, and one of the principal Indians, or at any rate, considered as such, from the circumstance of his speaking the English language tolerably well, complained of the white people for springing and overturning his racoon traps, and observed in the Indian style, "if I catch white man throwing my trap, I kill him." He appeared considerably exasperated at the conduct of the whites, and seemed disposed to remedy the evil by resorting to revenge.[34]

In the days following this encounter, Hudson was given further reason to believe that Ludlow might pose a danger both to the property of whites and, what was much worse, to his wife and their small children. A few days after stumbling into Logan's camp for the first time, Hudson was asked to assist his neighbor, Miles Elliot, and Elliot's son, Seneca, in a search for missing cattle. Instead of stray livestock, their morning search led to the discovery of numerous tracks of Indian horses in the area where the cattle had been foraging. The Elliot family also maintained a sugar camp, and as Hudson passed through it on his way home, Mrs. Elliot stepped away from her syrup kettles long enough to pass on ominous news, observing:

> That Ludlow had been at my [Hudson's] house, in my absence, with a
> small basket, which he wanted my wife to take and demanded, by way
> of exchange, for it, four pounds of sugar—that she refused to do—
> that Ludlow treated her with abusive language—drew his knife twice
> and threatened to kill her in case of non-compliance; lest he might
> put his threats in execution, she gave him the sugar, and he went off.
> Ludlow, I was afterwards told, had been drinking spirits.[35]

Returning to his home immediately after this unsettling encounter, Hudson found it empty. He found his wife at the home of his neighbor, Andrew Sawyer, where the story of Ludlow's threats was the topic of general conversation. "I left home, said she, for fear the Indian might return and kill me." Hudson, at the time, dismissed the remark with a laugh.

Meanwhile, there is reason to believe that Harper and Bridge had also had a number of confrontations with Ludlow. It is impossible to say whether Harper, or any of the whites, were in fact disturbing the traps of the Indians, as Ludlow angrily alleged. It is, however, easy to imagine Harper, the propertyless, Indian-hating newcomer, upsetting the traps of the Indian band. Trapping success, which furnished a sellable and essentially liquid commodity, would have been of considerably greater importance to a man of Harper's background than to the settled farmers, regardless of his feelings about the Indians. Ensuring that success by eliminating the competition from Indian traps may have struck Harper as a well-considered strategy.

But there is no need to resort to speculations of this sort to trace the emergence of a mortal hostility between Harper and Bridge and Ludlow. Harper, allegedly surprised that a band of Indians had camped so close to his relations, persuaded Bridge to accompany him on a visit to Logan's camp in the days before the killings. While there, according to the accounts of Bridge's descendants, "one of the Indians" displayed to the two men scalps that were claimed to have been taken from whites. If this is in fact the case, it is most unlikely that the Indian in question was Logan, who was renowned for his friendship for the whites, but rather one of the two younger men, Ludlow or M' Doal. And given Ludlow's facility with English, and the other accounts that suggest he had a fiery (and in this case, foolhardy) streak, it seems likely that he, and not M' Doal, would have been the one to flaunt such trophies.

Hudson mentions neither such a visit, of which he conceivably had no knowledge, nor the display of scalps by the Indians. He does, however, record a chilling incident suggesting that the elder Bridge, a man with no reputation as a particular hater of Indians, had also come to believe that Logan's people were a threat and that he was willing to take the most drastic measures to remove them. Three days before the murders, Hudson was passing time at Bridge's farm, shooting at targets with Harper. In the course of their competition, according to Hudson, Bridge returned from a visit to Doctor Hiday (sometimes spelled Hidy or Highday), a prominent early settler and possibly the community's first medical professional. The doctor had provided Bridge with a powder, whose purpose Bridge did not describe, but which Hudson believed was a poison meant for the Indians:

> I am, however, of opinion that his principal object in going thither was to procure poison for the purpose of destroying the Indians; and from the best information I could obtain, it was put into whiskey for the purpose of effecting that object. Good whiskey was first offered them, but as few would partake, (it being then their hunting season) it was deemed advisable to abandon this course.[36]

Like Logan's refusal to drink on the morning of his death, this episode provides more evidence that the Indians could, at times, easily resist the lure of liquor. More importantly, Bridge's evil scheme and the apparent complicity of Hiday suggest that a fatal animosity had already infected members of the white community far beyond the circle of the eventual killers.

And then there is the mysterious, suggestive allusion to crooked business dealings in the confrontational encounter between Ludlow and Harper on the morning of the killings. While conversing with the Indians prior to their fatal walk in the woods, as Hudson recalled, "Ludlow . . . enquired of one of our party, the reason why a dog he had bought of Harper, had been taken from him, and appeared angry at thus being deprived of his property, particularly as he received no satisfactory answer."[37]

What are we to make of this incident, which Hudson thereafter dismisses without elaboration? It is impossible to be sure. It is entirely plausible, however, to imagine that a hardened racist such as Harper had few compunctions about perpetrating fraud on a band of Indians. Perhaps he had at some point fobbed off a neighbor's dog as his own, selling it to the unsuspecting Ludlow, who then had to deal with the animal's recovery by aggrieved or angry settlers, while being naturally resentful and bitter because he had been cheated himself. And Ludlow's resentment, which he expressed in open musings about killing the white men, according to Hudson, was clearly a threat that was known to Harper.

Taken as a whole, this string of events suggests that later accounts emphasizing the acceptance of the "inoffensive" Indians by the white community seriously misconstrue the actual climate of settler opinion in some quarters. It points, instead, to a volatile atmosphere of growing hostility between some of the Indians and a considerable portion of the settler community. Admittedly, this conclusion rests upon a slender base of evidence—Hudson's confession and the ex post facto account of a descendant of one of the killers. Is there any reason to believe Hudson's testimony?

Perhaps. In the first place, let us suppose Hudson, from a desire to exculpate himself, lied by insinuating that the killings were not mere random violence, but a response to legitimate fears prompted by threatening behavior by the Indians. Why not lie about Logan rather than Ludlow? At the time of his confession, after all, Hudson had been tried, convicted, and was awaiting execution not for the fate of Ludlow, but for his murder of Logan. In all his melodramatic account, however, while freely admitting his guilt and repeatedly expressing remorse, he never once attributes a threat, act of violence, expression of anger, or other aggressive behavior to his victim Logan, to M' Doal, or to any of the other Indians. Only Ludlow. And it is easy to imagine Ludlow, a man of mixed race and a man suspended between two worlds, becoming truculent in his insistence upon his equality with the condescending and cheating whites. Even if he suspected that lies about Logan would be unavailing, since Logan as it turns out had a reputation for friendliness to whites, Hudson might still have insinuated that M' Doal had behaved in ways that had "provoked" some of the whites. But he did not do so.

What of Thurman's testimony about arguments and hostile incidents that preceded the killings? Superficially, there are good reasons to suspect her story. She freely admits that she is out to correct what she views as a one-sided historical record. "This article is written with no intention to vindicate the murders of 1824," she declares, "but it seems only fair when any crime of a past period is being reviewed to make public all the things that have a bearing on the situation."[38] So, it is possible that her reliability is fatally compromised by her admittedly revisionist intent. However, while not citing Hudson's confession, and while giving no evidence that she had even heard of its existence, she seems to confirm Hudson's testimony about the building antagonism between Logan's band and the settlers.

"There is also a tradition that a settler's wife had been attacked by an Indian," she writes. Thurman then dismisses the story, in a way that suggests her lack of familiarity with Hudson's account. "It is more likely that this is what they feared would happen rather than what had actually taken place for no evidence of the kind is presented at the trial according to the records."[39] Although vague, this statement confirms that the traditions she relied upon had at least some conformity with the perceptions of major actors at the time, as recorded in Hudson's account written more than a century earlier.

A simmering atmosphere of suspicion and anger, fraud, and alleged death threats, all poisoning relations between Logan's band and many local whites, was the apparent situation on Friday, March 19, 1824, when Harper, Andrew Sawyer, Hudson, and many other whites gathered for a house-raising at the farm of Peter Jones. The men worked, gossiped, and passed around the jug, until conversation "turned upon the subject of the Indians hunting in, and making disturbance in the neighborhood."[40]

When Hudson raised the matter of Ludlow's threats against Phebe, it triggered a violent, spontaneous outburst throughout the group. One member of the company commented, "that if an Indian would draw a knife upon his wife he would kill him." No doubt enflamed and emboldened by drink, the men enthusiastically agreed. Then Harper spoke up and "swore that all the Indians ought to be killed—Andrew Sawyer said that if an Indian would steal a horse from him, he would shoot him if possible." Discussion of the Indians—"all of which was of an unfavorable character"—continued until the working party broke up in the afternoon.[41]

Here was the genesis of the mass killings three days later. Clearly, a substantial portion of the community, in the eyes of men such as Harper, Sawyer,

Bridge, and Hudson, had implicitly agreed that the Indians were a menace against whom the most extreme measures were justified. It was the very afternoon of this house-raising that Hudson met Bridge returning with poison from the home of Hiday. That night, he recalled, he heard gunfire from the direction of Sawyer's sugaring camp and developed a powerful fear that the Indians "might come under the cover of night and destroy my family."[42]

The following Sunday was the eve of the killings. Hudson that morning returned to Jones's new home to attend Sabbath preaching. Hearing more gunfire, Hudson and his wife hurried home in fear that their children were in danger. This was not the case, but shortly after their return they were paid a visit by Sawyer. "Hudson, I want you to go out with me this evening. I think the Indians have stolen my horses," he declared. "The two colts have come running up without the mares, and the Indians must have taken them."[43]

Hudson set out immediately, with Sawyer and five others, including Bridge Sr., his sons James and John Jr., Harper, and Andrew Jones. The men searched until darkness and did not recover the horses. They did, however, make a discovery that Hudson said convinced him that the Indians were in fact horse thieves. At a short distance from the Indian camp, the search party discovered two small piles of corn, which they concluded must have been set out by the Indians as lures to help them snare Sawyer's missing horses. At dark, as the rain began to pour down, the men split up, agreeing to resume the search in the morning. Hudson stayed the night at Sawyer's home.

The following morning, the two were joined at Sawyer's by Harper, Peter and Andrew Jones, and the three Bridge men. Over their breakfast, Harper and Sawyer excited the passions of the others with further threatening talk and tales of Indian treachery. Harper told the story of the killing of his brother by Indians during the last war. Sawyer reiterated his threats from the house-raising three days before and boasted again that he was going to kill the Indians if the horses were found in their possession.

In this mood of barely controlled violence, the band of men set off for the Indian camp along Deer Lick Creek. Hudson, at least, still seems to have believed they were looking for horses. In fact, they were now a war party. At several points along the way, Hudson saw Harper and Sawyer exchange quiet words with other men in the group, which he later assumed to be planning for their resolution to kill the Indians whether they were involved with the alleged horse theft or not. Hudson's subsequent assumption was probably correct. In the minds of Sawyer, Harper, Bridge, and the others, the community approved of their plan. To the generalized hatred of all Indians that some of them clearly felt was now added the belief these specific Indians disturbed the community economically and threatened it as a manifest physical menace.

Some in the white community seemed to have already indicated their tacit support for the elimination of the Indians. And to all these inducements, some of the men would have added the attractions of enriching themselves with the property of the dead Indians while avenging the murder of their relatives. In the minds of the killers, the violence they were preparing to wreak would not be an attack on a band of harmless and innocent civilians, but an act of vengeance and reprisal for past Indian offenses and a preemptive strike against a dangerous threat to the community.

Given such incentives, and the ways in which the whites had already justified in their own minds violence against Logan, Ludlow, and the other Indians, the brutality of the murders is perhaps not so surprising. Approaching the Indian camp that morning, "murder in their hearts," some probably believed that the community would approve their actions. They would discover, to their dismay, that they were mistaken. And this fatal miscalculation was compounded by another misjudgment: despite their butchery at the camp, which they believed had covered their crime and deflected suspicion, the white men had left a witness to their crimes.

4

Damage Control
State and Settlers after the Killings

"For where there is no one in control nothing useful or distinguished can ever get done. This is roughly true of all departments of life."[1]
XENOPHON

Thomas Harper and his accomplices were mistaken in their belief that Madison County's white community would sanction, or at least ignore, the killing of the Indians at the Big Lick and at Deer Lick Creek. In fact, the rampage through the hunting camp exposed deep divisions of feeling in the community. Despite the brutality of the murders, many whites in Madison County and nearby communities sympathized with the killers and rallied to their support, engaging high-powered legal assistance and circulating impassioned clemency petitions. Many others, however, responded to the carnage with incredulous shock and outrage.

The killers anticipated the attitude of the authorities with even less accuracy. While a handful of government officials, especially at the state and local level, reacted to the killings with a lethargy that might suggest some sympathy with the murderers, the typical response was precisely the opposite—a surprisingly determined and active pursuit, apprehension, and prosecution of the killers.

Those who favored stern punishment for the offenders believed that there was a great deal at stake. Spontaneous popular violence clearly threatened to undermine social control and public order, especially when it was unprovoked, as appeared to be the case at Fall Creek. It was also expensive in several ways. Public funds would have to be spent to maintain the peace in the detention and prosecution of the alleged perpetrators. Far graver, however, was the potential economic damage of such violence. A booming local market in land, steadily appreciating in value, was the key generator of capital on the frontier.

For the average pioneer, to say nothing of the well-to-do speculating class, the appreciation of real estate was the only available investment resembling the stock market or mutual funds of the present day. If the threat of violence deterred settlement, Indiana's primary engine of growth faced a catastrophic setback. The same was true, in a slightly less immediate way, of the loss to anticipated wealth from the development of Indiana's agricultural and natural resources.

Men such as Harper, James Hudson, or John T. Bridge Sr. and his sons may have been unlikely to reflect on these short- and long-term economic consequences of their berserk rampage, but local government officials were quite sensitive to any blow, real or imagined, to their wallets. Traders, speculators, and prosperous farmers in the local gentry felt the same, and both groups acted promptly. But such obvious material concerns should not be allowed to obscure the role played by genuine outrage. Mingled with fear and worry, many frontiersmen expressed a sincere revulsion against the perpetrators of such heinous violence. From the evidence that survives, in newspaper accounts, in memoirs, and in the verdicts of the local juries, it seems clear that many, perhaps most, local whites were appalled by the murders.

As news of the incident spread, a posse of armed, angry farmers joined Madison County lawmen who were moving to arrest the suspected killers. At the same time, federal bureaucrats in charge of relations between the United States and local Indian tribes prodded the national government to intervene in the prosecution of the crime. Throughout the last days of March and early April, however, sympathizers and accusers alike labored beneath an almost palpable cloud of fear that violent Indian retribution seemed likely. In the days after the discovery of the killings, as evidence against Harper and his accomplices mounted, panic spread through the scattered and vulnerable white community of the New Purchase.

Apprehension and Flight

The designs of the killers unraveled within a day of the murders. The gory mutilation of the Indian corpses luridly recounted in all the stories of the affair was intended, according to Hudson's allegation and the belief of others at the time, to suggest that the deeds were the work of drunken Indians. As has been seen, this was not an entirely unreasonable stratagem. M' Doal was gone, perhaps in hiding with other Indians in the woods, or dead of his wounds. The bodies of Logan and Ludlow were concealed in shallow forest graves, far from the muddy pool that held the remains of the butchered women and children. The unexplained disappearance of all the band's adult males would puzzle other settlers. Knowing the frontiersman's belief that Indian warriors were prone to frenzies of inebriated violence, there was a certain shrewdness to the killers' calculations about the conclusions their neighbors would be likely to reach.

If this was really the intent of Harper and his accomplices—if in taking knives, hatchets, and a hominy pounder to the bodies of the dead, they were trying to implicate drunken Indians, rather than simply indulging a proclivity for racist atrocity—the effort was yet another miscalculation. No one seems to have been fooled by such ham-fisted subterfuge. It says a good deal about Harper's reputation as an Indian hater, and perhaps about the regard in which the Madison County settler community held many of his Bridge and Sawyer relations, that they appear to have attracted the immediate suspicion of their neighbors. Nor was a sense of this suspicion the only psychological freight weighing down the killers. The possible narrow escape of M' Doal from the site of the carnage had to have troubled Harper, Hudson, and the others. Uncertain of his fate, they were harried by worries that he might tell what he had seen to white authorities, or, even worse, relay the news to vengeful Indians in the vicinity.

Guilt was not a burden they bore lightly. With the possible exception of Harper, the killers were boys and family men, not habitual reprobates or hardened criminals. This is precisely the most chilling and ultimately inexplicable aspect of the entire affair. What explains their barbaric deviation from the normal standards of conduct to which these men seem to have adhered throughout their lives? The race hatred clearly evident in the character of Harper was only a partial explanation. In part, the killers shared a genuine fear that Logan's band constituted a threat. They also expected that violence against the Indians would meet with the tacit approval of the community. In the case of John Bridge Jr., parental and peer pressures may have been decisive. Bad company, an excess of liquor that impaired judgment and relaxed inhibition, and sheer brutal stupidity played a role as well.

Whatever the variety and relative weight of their motivations, most of the killers were clearly not up to bearing the emotional burden of their actions. Awareness of guilt, and perhaps the gnawing doubt about M' Doal, worked quickly on their nerves, which undermined their efforts to hide their complicity. Over the course of the day following the murders, they behaved in increasingly erratic fashion. By a series of awkward attempts to direct suspicion to imaginary Indian perpetrators, as well as brutal remarks about the Indians at the camp, they aroused the suspicion of their neighbors and ultimately incriminated themselves.

The first to expose his guilt to outsiders was Bridge Sr., the oldest of the killers. Bridge returned home from the Indians' hunting camp accompanied by his sons and Harper. All these men must have been emotionally spent from their morning's bloodletting. In addition, this psychic exhaustion would have been compounded for several by the depression and physical discomfort that follow prolonged, heavy consumption of alcohol. After soaking up whiskey all weekend at the Jones house-raising and at the hunting cabin in an effort to steel their nerves as they prepared for the killings, they undoubtedly would have been feeling the debilitating aftereffects of binge drinking.

At their cabin they found fifteen-year-old John Adams, a son of their neighbor, Abraham Adams.[2] The boy had been sent to the Bridge homestead around midday to purchase a bag of corn for his father. He spent the raw, rain-soaked afternoon shelling corn by the fire with two of the Bridge children and then dozed off at the hearthside, his sack of corn for a pillow. Awakened by the entry of Harper and the Bridges, he noted "something very strange in their appearance." Feigning sleep, he lay listening to the men talk and slowly began to suspect that they had been killing Indians.[3] Later, when the others barred the door and retired, he drifted back to sleep.

On the morning after the killings, March 23, the elder Bridge roused young Adams and sent him back to his father with a message: the Indians out at the hunting camp had very probably taken their neighbor Sawyer's horses. Bridge asked that Abraham should come, armed, to help hunt for them. He also remarked, as young Adams departed, that he had heard disturbances the night before, and he believed there might be something wrong at the Indian camp.[4]

John obeyed Bridge, returning home and conveying the message to his father. But he also noted Bridge's late return the day before and told his father of the sinister remarks he had overheard. Moved by the boy's distraught manner, the elder Adams did as Bridge asked. Taking a rifle, Adams returned with John to the Bridge farm. The two set out from there in the company of Bridge, two of his sons, and Harper.

The party proceeded through the woods to the Sawyer farm, a mile or so north of the Indian camp. Here they found not only the Sawyer family, but also Hudson, who had left his wife early that morning to make his way to Sawyer's cabin. Seeking out the company of his partners in crime, Hudson was helping Sawyer and his son split shingles for their roof. At the approach of the Bridge party, Andrew Sawyer laid aside his tools, telling the men there was no further need to seek the horses. Although the two mares had returned home on their own the previous evening, he was worried because "his boys had heard a heavy firing out at the Indian camps and [he] was suspicious that the Indians had been killing one another."[5]

Thus, within a day of the slaughter, two of the killers, Sawyer and Bridge, had told Adams they thought some mischief must have taken place at the Indian camp. At least one of them had suggested that the Indians themselves might have inflicted violence upon one another. Adams, apparently, was not taken in by such overt efforts to arouse and direct his suspicions. The Adamses and the party who had committed the murders then set off southward through the dense, sodden woods to investigate the Indian camp.

Approaching the campsite, Abraham Adams was struck by an unsettling silence. The predictable domestic din that had always greeted him in previous visits to Logan's campsite—barking dogs, clamorous children, women's voices—was entirely absent. This in itself was strange, but the eerie quiet acquired a more sinister aspect when Adams saw the appearance of the camp. Stepping into the midst of the wigwams, he noted that no fires were burning, neither for cooking nor to fend off the damp March chill. The site, to his initial bewilderment, appeared to have been suddenly and unexpectedly deserted.

Then he noted what appeared to be bloodstains on the ground in a number of places. The campsite was also strewn with other unidentifiable but suspicious-looking objects. Upon closer examination, he realized with revulsion that these shapeless pieces of debris were bits of mangled flesh, fragments of bone, and other organic tissue that he took to be brain. Bridge Sr. again attempted to imply Indian perpetrators, suggesting to Adams that "perhaps the Indian men had come home drunk and murdered their women and children."[6]

These nauseating discoveries were succeeded by an even more horrible find. Following a path a short distance through the woods, Adams and the other men came upon the flooded "hog wallow" filled with naked, bloody, disfigured corpses. Wriggling in their midst, to their stunned horror, Adams and the killers discovered one woman, bleeding and battered, but alive. Clinging to life through the night, this survivor is variously described as "half-white" (by Hudson) and as a "squaw of about fourteen" in other accounts. All agree, however, that she tried to utter a few halting words in English and some Indian language. She may very well have been the woman who pleaded in vain for the lives of the Indians immediately before the killings on the previous day.

> It was a sight at which cruelty itself shuddered—she was partly in the water—naked—she could speak but few words of English and these were indistinct—they were uttered with groans, which had their origin in her wounds—sobs which emanated from the heart for the loss of her relatives, and fear from the reappearance of the ministers of death. Many of the party did not approach to view this dreadful picture of destruction[7]

As the group contemplated this horrific spectacle, Bridge Sr. broke their stunned silence by declaring that "she ought to be killed out of her misery."[8]

His barbaric suggestion was ignored. While the white men declined Bridge's fiendish proposal to euthanize the only known survivor of the previous day's violence, their behavior reveals the chilling indifference with which many of the settlers regarded Indian suffering. Scattering from the camp to spread the alarm through the county, Adams and the others unbelievably simply abandoned the woman in the hog wallow. Barely more than a child, the woman had miraculously survived the white gang's crazed killing spree. Somehow, she withstood a night of exposure to rain and near-freezing temperatures and endured the traumatic horror of a day among the corpses in the flooded hole. Now, with her seeming rescue at hand, she was left alone to suffer throughout that Tuesday and until the next morning, two days after the attack on the camp.

Incredibly, when an investigating party arrived at dawn on Wednesday, the woman was still clinging to life. After leaving the hunting camp in shocked horror, Adams and his son alerted the small public safety bureaucracy of the newly incorporated county, consisting of Coroner Charles Tharp and Sheriff Samuel Cory. Tharp and about a dozen men, constituting a coroner's inquest, returned to the camp to investigate, nearly forty-eight hours after the killings. The party included Conrad Crosley, who had pursued a slander charge against Sawyer some months earlier, and Adam Winchell and Samuel Holliday, two of the judges elected to the local circuit court who would later hear cases involving the murders.[9]

It is difficult for the modern reader, trying to accurately reconstruct the events at Fall Creek, to gauge the significance of this lone and improbable survivor. Does it mean, for example, that the brutality of the killings was exaggerated or sensationalized at the time? All the earliest accounts emphasize the post-killing mutilation of the dead. "Their bodies were most shockingly mangled," the *Indianapolis Gazette* reported on the thirtieth, "for the purpose of producing an impression that it was the work of Indians, and thrown into a hole of water occasioned by the falling of a tree."[10] Is it reasonable to suppose that a "shockingly mangled" young woman, presumably also suffering from at least one gunshot wound, could survive two days and nights of shock, without food and clean water, while she lay naked and bleeding in the cold and damp?

If not, there may be other explanations for the insistence of local lore on the ghoulish treatment of the dead by the killers. Whatever the results of Tharp's impromptu inquest, no official report of his findings appears to have been filed, or at least to have survived. Understandably shocked by what they saw, the first discoverers may have exaggerated the extent of the violation wrought on the dead. Or perhaps the killers, in the orgy of violence that overtook them after apparently killing all of the women and children, actually inflicted less posthumous violence than they and others believed. Language matters as well. "Mangling" and "mangled" are evocative but vague terms, and they were customarily invoked in the literature of that day, along with the word "massacre," to convey a sense of heinous injury.[11] The young Indian woman's improbable survival, however, suggests that "mangle" in the context of frontier massacre narratives may be more a trope than a reliable description.

Whatever the nature and extent of her wounds, the woman's fate in the hands of Tharp and the other white authorities was little better than if she had been abandoned to a slow death at the camp. After examining the wigwams and the hog wallow, the party also located Logan's body, examining his wounds and interring him. It is not clear whether Ludlow's corpse was ever discovered. Tharp, Cory, and the other members of the inquest then took the surviving woman away to seek aid.

Their first stop was at the farm of Peter Jones. At this place five days earlier, during Jones's house-raising, the seeds of the massacre were planted as the killers worked themselves into anger by venting their outrage against the Indians. Just three days earlier, on the morning before the killings, Hudson and many other settlers had attended preaching, Bible reading, and Sabbath services at this very farm. Now, Jones refused to have the woman in his home.

Jones's stunning lack of Christian charity apparently evoked no remonstrance from his neighbors, but it did elicit a response from Bridge, who offered to shelter the battered but semiconscious woman in his home. Incredibly, despite the fact that he had just proposed to finish her off and that some already suspected that Bridge was involved in the killings, the woman was placed in the Bridge cabin. There is no indication that medical help was sought from Doctor Hiday. This, presumably, was just as well. Unsurprisingly, on the following morning, the girl was found dead in the Bridge home, "marks of violence upon her person."[12]

While this tenacious but helpless survivor awaited her beastly fate at the hands of the Bridges, the wheels of the Madison County law enforcement apparatus began to turn. Although Cory appears to have had no officially appointed deputies, the county did have a militia, consisting of twenty-two men under the command of Major John Montgomery. At Cory's request, the major called up his forces, and during the night of Wednesday, March 24, they surrounded the Bridge home—where Harper was also residing—with a round-the-clock guard. Harper, it appears, exhibiting either remarkable stupidity, brazen disregard for community suspicion, or a little of both, had already been seen with quantities of Indian goods, including leggings and moccasins, strapped to his horse. Furthermore, as Hudson confessed, "From conduct and movements of all engaged in this affair, suspicion immediately rested upon us."[13]

At daylight on March 25 the authorities closed in. Montgomery's militia, aided by other settlers including Cory and county clerk Moses Cox, moved to take Harper and the Bridges into custody. They were, unfortunately, not quite quick enough. While the younger Bridge was promptly seized, both Harper and Bridge Sr. fled. Cox and other armed citizens gave determined chase, firing as their two suspects desperately sped away on foot, sprinting downhill from the back of the Bridge cabin. For Bridge, the effort to escape was the old story of a willing spirit betrayed by the weakness of the flesh. The balding, middle-aged farmer lacked the requisite speed and nimbleness of foot. Stumbling down the hill and falling to the ground, though uninjured, he was promptly set upon and taken by his pursuers.

Harper was a different matter altogether. Of a naturally more extreme disposition than Bridge, younger by some years, athletically built, and "being an active man," he managed to elude his pursuers. Momentarily narrowing the gap when Harper slowed to scale a fence, they resolved to take desperate measures rather than lose their suspect. Cox and other members of the citizens' posse took aim and delivered a ragged volley from a number of rifles as he went over. Harper, uttering a cry, seemed to fall to the ground. Frontier marksmanship, however, failed in this crucial moment. To the disappointment of his pursuers, Harper had not been hit, and when they gained the fence themselves they saw him continuing his flight without injury—some said he covered eighty miles through the forests that day. No one in Madison County ever saw him again. Thus, gunfire ringing in his ears, the seething instigator of the murders eluded worldly justice, vanishing as abruptly as he had appeared.[14]

The fate of Harper remains one of the greatest of the many riddles surrounding the Fall Creek episode. Depending upon which source one chooses to credit, he fled to Kentucky, Virginia, southern Ohio (where a reward was offered for his capture and a posse allegedly sought him for a time), or Texas, "the common refuge of all bad men."[15] The most unlikely story of his fate, perhaps, is that which appeared in a history of Butler County, Ohio, in 1882: "After the Indians were killed the civil authorities offered a reward for the capture of the Harpers, and one of the Ridges [sic], who gave his assistance, but they fled to Virginia. Here they were taken prisoner, but in time gained their liberty."[16]

Although Cory, Cox, and their posse botched the attempt to seize Harper, they had successfully apprehended the Bridges, father and son, leaving Hudson, Andrew and Stephen Sawyer, and Andrew Jones at large. Hudson and Jones were arrested at gunpoint the same afternoon, without incident. Arriving at the Sawyers', the authorities found Andrew retrieving deerskins, furs, and sundry other Indian valuables from beneath his cabin's floorboards, apparently preparatory to following Harper's example.[17] He had less luck than Harper, however, or the authorities exercised greater care in their descent upon the Sawyer farmstead, because both Sawyers were taken by the militia without complication. Thus, within three days of the killings, six of the gang of seven killers found themselves in the hands of the State.

The Conscience of John Johnston

Hysteria swept through Madison County and then throughout the northern half of Indiana. The tenuous sense of security that had been growing since statehood in the white community vanished overnight, and a spontaneous wave of terror rippled northward from Indianapolis, touching all the isolated farms and villages of the New Purchase.[18] News of the killings, recounted in graphic detail, was trumpeted by the region's fledgling press, from Richmond in the north to Vincennes and Corydon in the south. Before the end of the month, the gruesome tale reached across the nation to the East Coast.[19]

The episode evoked a host of grim specters from the previous decade. Many were certain that this new butchery would reignite the hit-and-run guerrilla raids—the nightmare of scalping, burning, and abductions—that swept over them during the War of 1812. Madison County's sprinkling of white families fled their vulnerable homesteads, crowding for shelter into the hastily fortified mill at the falls of Fall Creek, in Pendleton, the tiny county seat. Some went further by sending their families out of the state for safety.[20]

They were quite right to be afraid. However quaint such fears may seem from the secure perspective of two centuries, the threat of Indian retaliation on a large scale was very real. Wars had begun over just such incidents within living memory. "Lord Dunmore's War" exploded in 1774 when a band of white land speculators, led by Michael Cresap, murdered a friendly Indian hunting party, unleashing a confederation of furious Delaware, Shawnee, Wyandotte, and Seneca braves onto the warpath in quest of revenge.[21] White pioneers knew that thousands of Miami, Seneca, and even a few Delaware—said to be the fiercest and most implacable of the tribes of the Northwest—still inhabited the northern part of the state, and several other hunting bands that included Indian warriors were believed to lurk in the vicinity of Madison County.[22]

Word of the killings spread among the local Indians at least as quickly as it ran through the white community, and tribal leaders were, in fact, furious. They were also fearful that they would be unable to restrain tribal demands for bloody vengeance. The custom in cases of murder or manslaughter among most tribes of the region was to maintain order by requiring physical retribution or payment to the family of the victim, but it was clear that monetary compensation alone would be insufficient in this case. "As soon as the murder was known among the Indians," a local source reported, "many of whom were in the neighborhood hunting, they declared if the murderers were not secured and punished, satisfaction would fall upon innocent persons, as they could not restrain their young men."[23]

As events unfolded, however, the war clouds vanished almost as quickly as they had gathered, and peace and public order were maintained on the Hoosier frontier. Given the situation at the time, the fallout from the massacre was controlled about as well as any reasonable observer could have hoped

Little Turtle, a Miami chief, led a confederacy that achieved military success over U.S. military forces in the 1790s.

or expected. This fact was due almost entirely to the intervention of a single, remarkably humane, accomplished, and largely forgotten public servant, John Johnston, the U.S. Indian agent in nearby Piqua, Ohio.

At the time of the murders on Fall Creek, few white men in the Northwest Territory disposed of a greater fund of knowledge and experience in dealing with the region's native tribes. Born in 1775 of Scottish ancestry in County Donegal, Ireland, Johnston was brought to North America at the age of eleven to settle in Pennsylvania. He was hardworking and ambitious. In his teens he left home to go west as a teamster in Anthony Wayne's Indian campaign in Ohio. He served in Wayne's supply column at the Battles of Fort Recovery and Fallen Timbers in 1794, and he witnessed in the same year the signing of the Treaty of Greenville, by which most of Ohio was ceded to the United States. When the fighting ended, he took a post as a clerk in the War Department in Philadelphia. His ability and diligence were noted. At the age of twenty-seven, Johnston was sent by the department to take over the U.S. government factory at Fort Wayne, where he commenced his duties on July 1, 1802.

Johnston spent ten years as the factor at Fort Wayne. The "factories" were the brainchild of George Washington. Established by act of Congress in 1795, the factories developed into a network of government-run trading houses with the tribes. The system's success was uneven, and it always had many critics who decried the corruption of some agents. Thomas Jefferson, however, was a fervent believer who worked aggressively to expand these outlets of subsidized exchange.

Jefferson saw in the factories both a means of "civilizing" the Indians by increasing their dependency on the whites and a tool to drive out rapacious, private traders who often caused friction with the tribes. Over the next quarter century, twenty-eight such trading posts were established, nearly all in conjunction with, indeed, often within the precincts of, a frontier military post. As factor, Johnston earned one thousand dollars per year, for which he managed the factory's considerable inventory, supervised daily trade, and advised the local military officers in their struggle to maintain the brittle peace along the northwest frontier.[24]

Johnston's status as factor made him the official business liaison between the American government and the local tribes. Relations in a more strictly political sense, however, were typically handled by another federal appointee, the "Indian agent." These officials were the bureaucratic descendants of the pre-Revolutionary era's colonial agents and the earlier British supervisors of In-

Anthony Wayne's victory at Fallen Timbers (1794) ended Native American resistance in Ohio.

dian relations. Congress through trade and intercourse acts in 1790 and 1793 established the Indian agent in American law. The agent was both a reporter, who was expected to keep his superiors in the War Department advised of the state of Indian-white relations in the district for which he was responsible, and a sort of permanent facilitator of relations between local whites and the surrounding Indian tribes.

When the young Johnston was appointed to the Fort Wayne factory in 1802, the Indian agent there was William Wells, a controversial figure charged by Johnston and many others with defrauding the government of annuities meant for the Indians. The accusations against Wells were disputed, and Wells himself made similar allegations against Johnston. Neither man's incriminations were ever thoroughly investigated, but whatever the merit of those against Wells, they were sufficiently serious that in 1809 Johnston was appointed to replace him, taking on the dual role of both factor and agent for the government. Some of the credit for Johnston's appointment undoubtedly belongs to his friendship with another old Indian fighter from the days of the Wayne campaign, William Henry Harrison, now governor of the Indiana Territory. Two years later Johnston was appointed to the Indian agency at Piqua, Ohio, remaining until 1830 when the election of Andrew Jackson, whose political persuasion Johnston did not share ("the tyrant Jackson," as Johnston apostrophized him), ended his service.[25]

When Johnston left for Fort Wayne, the War of 1812 was brewing. In a sordid business that tarnished nearly all its practitioners, Johnston had apparently managed his responsibilities as Indian agent with unusual and unbending integrity. The factory system as it was run in the Old Northwest offered a rich variety of possibilities for fraud. Local traders, for example, could sell goods to the Indians on credit, and then present inflated bills to the factor for repayment out of the annuities due to the tribes. Or the Indian agent himself, charged with purchasing cattle, hogs, and horses for the Indians, could easily pad his costs when he submitted them to the War Department for remuneration.

Johnston, whose work was scrutinized on a number of occasions, appears to have maintained his integrity, as well as the profitability of his operation at Fort Wayne. It was said that Johnston's post was the most profitably run of all the U.S. agencies having yielded nearly ten thousand dollars of profit under his management.[26] By the time he left the post to his successor, the annual meeting of traders and Indians at the Fort Wayne Treaty Grounds drew up to one thousand people and had become "the greatest commercial event of northern Indiana."[27]

Johnston's performance earned him an appointment as quartermaster during the War of 1812, in which post he garnered further distinction. The ruddy, grey-eyed Johnston, known as "Colonel Johnston," though there is no record of his appointment to such rank, was a lithe fellow who matched a ramrod bearing with a stern Episcopalian temperament. He conceived of his duty as a public servant in a way that transcended party, and he deplored the rise of increasingly bitter partisan politics that he witnessed in the 1820s. Decades later, when two of his sons departed for the Mexican War (both died in the conflict), Johnston's valediction was typically austere: "You are to know nothing of party or party men. Be faithful to your flag, and always remember that the first and last duty of a soldier is to keep a shut mouth and obey orders."[28]

Congress liquidated the troublesome factory system in 1822, but Johnston remained in the post of agent for nearly two decades at Piqua, which was located on the Great Miami River, about seventy miles northeast of Madison County. From Piqua he managed relations with seven tribes—Shawnee, Potawatomi, Wyandotte, Seneca, Muncie, Miami, and Delaware. These comprised at the time, by Johnston's estimate, about six thousand people, and for his exertions he received twelve hundred dollars annually, with a housing allowance and two servants.

Johnston grew into a man of considerable distinction and broad accomplishment during these years. He discovered and urged the preservation of the ancient Indian mounds of the Adena culture and provided anthropological artifacts as well as specimens of Indian remains to early cultural researchers who often looked to him as an expert on Woodland Indian languages and customs.[29] He helped, in 1824, to found Kenyon College. When Daniel Boone died in 1826, Johnston was one of the honorary pallbearers who accompanied the titan's remains from Kentucky to his final resting place in Virginia.

Over time, Johnston conceived a warm admiration for what he considered the dignity and honesty of the Indians under his care, and he clearly saw himself as a benevolent, paternal advocate on their behalf. He knew and befriended the renowned Cayuga chief Logan, known as "the great Mingo" (probably father, but possibly uncle, to the Logan killed at Fall Creek), describing him as "a man of splendid appearance, over six feet high, straight as a spear shaft, with a countenance as open as it was brave and manly . . . the best specimen of humanity ever met with, either white, red or black."[30] Though by no means

blind to the horrific brutality of Indian warfare—Johnston was no romantic—
he also consistently decried the depravity and provocative unscrupulousness
of many whites in their dealings with the Indians.

By the time of the events at Fall Creek, Johnston's sympathy for the
Indians led him to advocate a policy of removal: "I am free to declare, that in
my judgement there is no adequate remedy but removal to a country of their
own, where a suitable Government could be established over them. Whatever
speculative benevolence may urge to the contrary their race must perish under
the present management."[31]

The Indians themselves, the objects of Johnston's concern here, seem
to have viewed him, understandably, with mixed feelings. On the one hand,
sixteen Seneca chiefs wrote to President James Monroe and Secretary of War
John C. Calhoun in February of 1824, barely three weeks before the Fall Creek
killings, to urge that he be continued as Indian agent: "We have tried him more
than twenty years," they wrote. "We continue to love him."[32] Others, however,
could be critical. Delaware Chief William Anderson, who also favored removal
as the only way of preserving the cultural existence of his people, complained
that Johnston had left his people completely unprepared for the conditions
of removal when they left Ohio and Indiana for the West in March of 1821,
resulting in their descent to a condition near "utter starvation."[33]

Late in his life, negotiating the treaty that would remove the last of the
Wyandotte from Ohio in one of the final official acts of a half-century career in
public service, Johnston crossed paths with Charles Dickens. In one of the vi-
gnettes that made up his *American Notes*, the great writer recalled Johnston as
"a mild old gentleman, who had been for many years employed by the United
States Government in conducting negotiations with the Indians," and whose
views on the ultimate necessity of removal struck Dickens as both humane
and persuasive.[34]

It was to Johnston that Madison County's militia dispatched a courier,
Captain John Berry, to bear tidings of the killings. While Harper escaped, and
his clumsy henchmen blundered into the hands of the law, Berry galloped over
the trails from Pendleton to Piqua. Another Indian agent was resident within
Indiana at the time—John Tipton, a man of renown in his own right, who
now held Johnston's old post at Fort Wayne—but Johnston had jurisdiction
over dealings with most of the tribes along the White River.

Johnston was appalled by the news. "The incident, for cold blooded cruelty
baffles all description," he told his superior, Secretary of War John Calhoun,

John Johnston's Ohio estate.

"and in point of atrocity surpasses anything that has ever disgraced the settle-ment of this country."[35] This was from a man not ordinarily given to hyperbole, and who was familiar with some very ugly violence indeed.[36] To Johnston, the killings looked like the start of a potential national security crisis, unless the resident Indian population's demand for retaliation could be promptly ap-peased. Faced with a multitude of distractions—he battled fevers and illness throughout the spring and summer of 1824, and he was in the midst of a prolonged and successful defense against new allegations of misusing public funds—Johnston responded immediately. He dispatched notice of the affair to the War Department in Washington, and he set out with Berry for the falls on Fall Creek.[37]

Arriving among the jittery settlers at Pendleton, Johnston found himself confronted with a number of practical problems. First and foremost was the fact that the newly minted county had neither a jail nor a courthouse. The pris-oners were being held in a cabin under a guard of sheriff's deputies. Johnston promptly took matters in hand, authorizing the construction of a log jail, the appointment of guards to be reimbursed, if necessary, from federal funds, and the manacling of the prisoners.

Cory and his deputies quickly constructed a windowless, one-room jail of timbers "hewed square, so that each timber fitted close to the one upon which it rested," and surrounded it with a palisade of sharpened logs, sixteen feet high. Within, a guardhouse sheltered four deputies. This rude prison thus became the new county's first government structure. Hudson, the Bridges, and Andrew Sawyer had been taken to the farm of the town blacksmith, Adam Winchell, who manacled them hand and foot. Winchell, an associate judge on the circuit court, would later hear the trial of the prisoners whom he had shackled. Jones and Stephen Sawyer, who had apparently agreed to cooperate with the prosecution of the other prisoners, were released on bail.[38]

Technically, Johnston was a federal official without jurisdiction on the incorporated land of Madison County, which was now subject to the state of Indiana. The situation seemed to him an emergency, however, calling for extraordinary measures. Accordingly, he wrote the governor of the state, Wil-liam Hendricks, to urge a prompt and aggressive prosecution of the crime. Hendricks failed to respond until the end of June, nearly three months after Johnston's arrival in Madison County. Johnston also informed his superi-ors in the War Department and sought their support for his initiative. As he explained later in the spring, the technical irregularity of his intervention seemed justified, both by the inaction of the governor and the alarm spreading over the frontier. "No other measure," he assured the secretary of war, "would secure a semblance of justice and peace to the region."[39]

His superiors shared Johnston's assessment. A few days before the murders, on March 11, Calhoun created within the War Department a special bureau of Indian affairs, appointing Thomas L. McKenney as its head. The office assumed responsibility for the ordinary course of Indian affairs correspondence, and McKenney, a humanitarian and something of a dreamer with grand schemes for Indian education, concurred with Johnston's sense of the urgency. He assured Johnston of the full support of the War Department, even to the point of executing any whites found guilty.

This, in fact, was something like what McKenney wanted. Experience with similar killings throughout the Indiana frontier showed that the Indians, in McKenney's view, were too quick to accept money as a sufficient compensation.[40] "You will impress it upon the kindred and friends of the murdered Indians that the Govt would prefer to see them less willing to commute their loss for money, and more disposed to take the applications of the law in punishing the murderers as the satisfaction due to such deeds," he told Johnston. Some example of "such monsters" had to be made that would "deter others from deeds so horrible."[41]

By the time McKenney conveyed these sentiments to Johnston seven weeks after the killings, his blessings were already somewhat ex post facto. Battling chronic illness in heavy weather, Johnston had been indefatigable in visiting the Indians for miles in every direction from the settlement, making payments, assuring tribal leaders of the concern of the government and, above all, urging them to await satisfaction by permitting the white system of justice to run its course. For a man of his age, even one who, like Johnston, was accustomed to a physically strenuous life, this was taxing work over incredible terrain. The trip by horseback from Corydon to Indianapolis, for example, a distance of perhaps seventy miles as the crow flies, took six days in 1820.[42] Johnston never faltered, remaining constantly on the road for several weeks.

He did not travel alone. Setting out for the campfires of the Seneca, Miami, and other Indians scattered over northern Indiana and Ohio, Johnston was joined by another of the Indiana frontier's most knowledgeable Indian hands, the trader William Conner. Raised with his brother, John, among Christian Indians at Moravian missions, Conner was a trader as his father had been, and by 1824 one of the wealthiest early capitalists on the Indiana

Hoping to prevent an outbreak of violence in the aftermath of the slayings, John Johnston traveled extensively among the Indian camps, giving assurances that the murderers would be punished.

frontier. He was the possessor of a fine house and estate in Hamilton County, twenty miles from the site of the murders on Fall Creek, disposing of a fortune sustained by land rents, successful commercial and agricultural activities, and far-flung business connections. Conner's intimate knowledge of the local tribes also led to numerous occasions where he served as an intermediary between the region's tribes and local whites.

For twenty years, Conner lived as a friend among the Delaware, taking a Delaware wife, Mekinges, the daughter of Chief William Anderson. She bore him six children, two of whom later became chiefs in their own right, and he grew wealthy, trading doles of whiskey for Indian furs. When the Delaware were removed from Indiana in the late summer of 1820, Conner sent his wife and children away westward with their people. Remaining behind in Indiana, Conner prospered. He took a new, white wife, who in turn bore him ten more children, and he was eventually elected to the state legislature. Entirely at ease with the language and customs of the Indians of the region, Conner was an ideal partner in Johnston's pacification tour.[43]

Throughout the rainy spring of 1824, Johnston and Conner splashed over forest trails and forded swollen streams as they made their way from camp to camp in the wilderness. Johnston's colleagues at the War Department shared his sense of urgency. Fearing a bloody, expensive eruption of violence, they exhorted him to the utmost effort. In early May, Lewis Cass, governor of the Michigan Territory and Johnston's immediate superior in Indian affairs, told Johnston to do everything possible to encourage the Indians to trust white justice. "This murder is so horrible and unprovoked, that every proper measure ought to be taken to bring the perpetrators to condign punishment," Cass declared. He went on to note:

> The first object is to quiet any alarms of the frontier settlers and Indi-
> ans which might lead to mutual aggression and depredations. From
> an intimation in an Indiana paper, I am afraid some of the exposed
> inhabitants may have abandoned their settlements, and sought
> security by associating a number of families together. I hope this is
> not the fact, and if it is, I trust confidence can be easily restored. It is
> also necessary the *Indians* should be fully *satisfied* that this atrocious
> act has been committed by bad men, who are not countenanced by
> the government, nor by any of our respectable citizens. And that no
> proper measure will be neglected to bring them to punishment. As

far as possible, it will be proper to explain the nature of our laws. That they recognize no difference between a white man and an Indian.[44]

Cass concluded his admonitions to Johnston by assuring him of the department's support in whatever he should undertake to procure adequate prosecution counsel and to requite any expenses for witnesses.

Johnston and Conner were already hard at work fulfilling Cass's charge. They spent weeks crisscrossing the Ohio-Indiana border to visit the Indian camps, begging for patience and doling out cash and goods in their effort to pacify outraged Indian feeling. The most important of the visits was to the family of Logan at Lewis Town, just a short distance from Johnston's home at Piqua. Writing Calhoun in the third week of May, Johnston made it clear that the panic was not over—"The affair has thrown the whole frontier for 200 miles around into the greatest confusion"—but that he was confident that the Indians were willing to give the government's justice a chance. Through his deft sense for the feelings of the Indians, as well as through the distribution of the gifts customary on such occasions, Johnston told Calhoun that he had "procured their unanimous consent to submit the case to the decision of the County."[45]

For the time being, in the middle of May 1824, the frontier shuttle diplomacy of Johnston and Conner seemed to be working. Although the fears of white settlers continued to wax, according to Johnston's testimony, none of the local Indian bands had taken retaliatory vengeance. There was no telling whether the peace would hold, and Johnston assured Calhoun that it was widely believed the Indians were intransigent in their demand for reparation by death, writing that "Many of the people have moved away and those who remain are under continual dread nothing will satisfy the Indians but the execution of some or all of the murderers. We are now in hope that this will take place and confidence be again restored."[46]

It is unclear whether Johnston was referring to the confidence of the settlers in their security, or of the Indians in the benevolent intentions of the American government. Whichever was the case, by this point the peace of the frontier, as well as the fate of the killers, rested with the wisdom of the attorneys and judges of Indiana's Fifth Circuit sitting at Pendleton, in Madison County.

5

One Kind of Justice

"I trust the sequel of this trial will for once vindicate our character, and convince them that we have not one kind of justice for Red Men and another for ourselves."[1]

JOHN JOHNSTON TO THOMAS MCKENNEY, OCTOBER 1824

John Johnston was convinced that the peace of the frontier hung in the balance as he made his way through the forest in April and May. "We who are among the Indians daily," he told Lewis Cass, "are unanimously of the opinion that should the murderers escape, the Indians will glut their revenge on the exposed settlements on White River."[2] By May he also felt certain that his mission—pacify the Indians and make an example of the perpetrators—enjoyed the wholehearted backing of the federal government's most powerful figures. Among everyone in the Indian affairs bureaucracy, from the agent Johnston to the superintendents Thomas L. McKenney and Lewis Cass to Secretary of War John C. Calhoun in President James Monroe's cabinet, unity and resolve prevailed. The furor over the murders had to be quelled at any cost, up to and including capital punishment if necessary, to appease the local tribes.

Indiana politicians joined Johnston in hoping for a swift resolution to the affair, believing that only a verdict satisfactory to the Indians would preserve the budding economic promise of the Hoosier frontier. Writing Cass seven weeks after the murders, Johnston assured his superior that the local law officers were acting with commendable zeal, and that they enjoyed the support of the settlers. "The people from their fear of the retaliatory vengeance of the Indians are affording [the authorities] all the support of their power."[3] The political elite of Indiana appeared to reflect popular sentiment as described by

Johnston. Governor William Hendricks called for the satisfaction of justice, deploring the "deleterious effects of the case on [Indiana's] general prosperity," as he declared while the case was in trial.[4]

The matter seemed settled. At the local, state, and national levels, those in power agreed that the murders demanded prompt retributive justice. Yet, there is very good reason to conclude that Johnston was being far less than candid when he conveyed his sunny assessment of local harmony to Cass. In fact, he doubted the integrity of his allies in the county's law enforcement, whom he suspected of deliberate negligence in their guard duties. Moreover, he was deeply worried that the fashionable consensus in favor of a quick disposition of the killers might be derailed by forces sympathetic to the prisoners now languishing on the banks of Fall Creek.

His anxieties were well-founded. In retrospect, there can be no doubt that a broad sentiment of unexpressed popular support for the actions of Thomas Harper, James Hudson, and the other killers pervaded Madison County. Despite the inclination of some state and federal figures to placate outraged Indian feeling by sacrificing Harper's feckless henchmen, many Hoosiers were eager to provide material and emotional support for the killers. A generation earlier, William Henry Harrison had lamented the fact that a great many Hoosier pioneers "consider the murdering of Indians in the highest degree meritorious."[5] His words still held true in Madison County in 1824.

James Hudson Pays the Devil

For two weeks after their arrest, Hudson, Andrew Sawyer, John Bridge Sr., and John Bridge Jr. sat chained and festering in the windowless log cube at Pendleton, awaiting the spring session of the Madison Circuit Court. The garrulous, persuasive Oliver H. Smith obtained Sheriff Samuel Cory's permission to visit the accused in their squalid log pen. Employing the folksy eloquence that made him famous as a senator, the tireless "prince of the circuit riders" left a vivid description:

> When I first saw them they were confined in a square log jail, built
> of heavy beech and sugar-tree logs, notched down closely and fitting
> tight above, below, and on the sides. I entered with the sheriff. The
> prisoners were all heavily ironed, and sitting on the straw on the floor.
> Hudson was a man of about middle size with a bad look, dark eye,
> and bushy hair, about thirty-five years of age in appearance. Sawyer
> was about the same age, rather heavier than Hudson, but there was

MASSACRE OF INDIANS

In 1824, nine Indians were murdered by white men near this spot. The men were tried, found guilty and hanged. It was the first execution of white men for killing Indians.

ERECTED BY INDIANA SESQUICENTENNIAL COMMISSION 1966

A historical marker testifies to the significance of events in Madison County in 1824–25.

nothing in his appearance that could have marked him in a crowd, as any other than a common farmer. Bridge, sen., was much older than Sawyer; his head was quite grey, he was above the common height, slender, and a little bent while standing. Bridge, jr., was some eighteen years of age, a tall stripling.[6]

The spring session of the circuit court did not commence until the second week of April. When Indiana's circuit courts sat in the 1820s, courtroom business was directed by a presiding judge, elected by the state legislature, and two locally elected associate justices, known as "side judges." The presiding judge for the Fifth Circuit in the spring of 1824 was William Wick, who had arrived in Indiana from Pennsylvania two years earlier and, despite his youth, became the first attorney admitted to the bar in Madison County, garnering sufficient renown to gain the legislature's nod for the circuit bench. A tall, swarthy man, Wick had "hair as black as a ravine" and a bearing that denoted "intelligence of a superior order."[7] In 1824 he was at the start of a distinguished political career that later saw him elected secretary of state for Indiana and eventually a member of the Hoosier delegation to the U.S. House of Representatives.

He was also, in that wet April, a sick man. Unable to attend the sessions, which opened on the eighth and by state law ran for three days, the empanelling of a grand jury to consider indictments was left to Wick's two side judges, Adam Winchell and Samuel Holliday. Winchell, the blacksmith who had forged the manacles for the suspects, was illiterate, but considered "honest, rough, frank . . . without any pretensions to legal knowledge." In the context of Madison County at the time, the stolid blacksmith's traits of character far outweighed any lack of legal expertise. He was obviously esteemed by the county's electors.[8] Holliday, like Wick, was an attorney who had settled in Madison County two years earlier and was promptly elected associate judge by his neighbors.[9]

The grand jury, a party of eight headed by a local farmer named Amasa Makepeace, returned bills of indictment on April 9. Hudson, the two Bridges, Sawyer, and Harper were indicted for one murder; Hudson and Bridge Jr. for another; and Sawyer and Harper for another. This, to Johnston's considerable annoyance, was as far as the legal proceedings went for the time being.

Given Wick's illness and the brevity of the circuit court session, the trials of the indicted prisoners were postponed until the court's fall session, in the second week of October. Two of the men arrested in the murders remained free. Andrew Jones, who had been present at the murder of Logan, and Stephen Sawyer, who had accompanied Harper at the murder of Ludlow, turned state's evidence. Posting an eight hundred-dollar bond as insurance, they spent the summer awaiting the trial in freedom.[10]

Throughout the summer, the panicked families of Madison County slowly recovered from their fear of Indian reprisals and returned to their homes. Sightseers turned the palisaded log prison on Fall Creek into a local curiosity. Cory not only permitted visitors to come and view the site of the killers' incarceration, but also occasionally allowed parties into the jail to gawk at close range. Sandford C. Cox recorded seeing a young boy, vexed at missing a visit with his father, scaling the log pickets and dropping within the compound, with the guards watching, to have a look at the criminals. Finally ordered out by one of the guards, the boy "as nimbly as a squirrel mounted to the top of the picket, grinned defiance at the sentinel, and descended outside."[11]

This was far from the only evidence of an informality with the prisoners so pronounced as to suggest an indifference to their guilt on the part of some of the authorities. Johnston used federal funds to provide, among other items, whiskey for the raising of the jail and its log palisade, as well as whiskey for the guards, and it clearly heightened their lack of attentiveness to their duties. On a number of occasions throughout the summer, various prisoners escaped the makeshift jail and were recovered only at great expense. Sawyer, for example, escaped and could only be recaptured after a lengthy and intensive manhunt. Johnston put the cost for his apprehension by Cory and a team of deputies at one hundred dollars.[12]

Despite the incompetence of Madison County's law enforcement, Johnston was determined to keep the prisoners in place, rather than remove them to a more secure and professionally run prison, so as not to arouse Indian fears that they were being transferred in preparation for release. At the same time, such a policy required extraordinary vigilance on his part, which he exercised with sufficient skill to earn special praise, early in the summer, from Governor Hendricks. The local sheriff, Hendricks commented, "was strangely negligent of his duties and gave them liberties which would probably have ultimated in their escape but for some precautionary measure as you have adopted, and which will no doubt be highly approved."[13]

Whether incidental or deliberate, the bungling sentries along Fall Creek frustrated Johnston. The problem of negligent turnkeys was soon eclipsed, however, by his discovery of a much more ominous threat to the goal of conviction and execution. Someone had hired a team of seven attorneys to defend the prisoners. The obvious question—where did the money come from?—is impossible to answer with certainty, but whoever was footing the bills paid a great deal for the defense of the four suspects. Expert legal help on the Indiana frontier was not cheap—Johnston's records indicate that the chief prosecuting attorneys earned as much as five hundred dollars per case—and neither court records nor surviving private documents reveal who it was that put up the money to bring in seven of the most prominent lawyers in Indianapolis.

Although Johnston almost certainly knew who was backing the defense, he left an ambiguous record. In October 1824, shortly after Hudson's trial concluded, he reported to McKenney that their defense was funded by the killers themselves: "The four murderers had engaged seven attorneys, among whom were some of the ablest in the state."[14] Sixteen months later, however, in another report to McKenney, Johnston recorded that it was not Hudson and the others, but instead "friends of the prisoners [who] had engaged the ablest counsel at and near Indianapolis."[15] None of the surviving papers of the attorneys themselves, including the extensive correspondence and diaries of lead defender Calvin Fletcher, indicate the sponsor of the legal team.

It is possible, even likely, that some of the costs of the defense were borne directly by the defendants, as Johnston initially suggested. Sawyer, for example, owned a farm of eighty acres, and Madison County land records indicate that it was sold in early September of 1824.[16] This was during the period of Sawyer's pretrial incarceration, following his indictment and just four weeks before the beginning of the fall session of the circuit court, so it is reasonable to suppose that the sale was part of an effort to defray legal expenses. Sawyer's eighty-acre plot, however, could have generated around one hundred dollars at the very most, a sum far short of what was necessary to finance such a lavish defense.

The other prisoners, to judge from the surviving records, disposed of even fewer means. The indictments describe both Bridge and Hudson as "labourer," and they do not appear in the surviving land records as either buyers or sellers of Madison County land. They may have squatted, or, even less likely, rented, but in either case, they did not convert any real estate into liquid assets to cover their legal expenses. Also, as shall be seen, it is highly unlikely that the attorneys involved in the defense were working pro bono.

This lends plausibility to Johnston's implicit assertion that a large share of the defense costs were borne by sympathetic backers of the prisoners. Many neighbors of the defendants—Doctor Hiday is a good example—clearly shared the feeling that the Indians had been a threat. Although Sawyer had

had some quarrels with neighbors, this was far from unusual at the time, and Bridge seems to have enjoyed some respect in the community, judging from his election to the first grand jury assembled in the county. Scores of neighbors, representing a significant chunk of the county's residents at the time, later rallied to the defense of Bridge Jr. as well. The presence of the distinguished defense team, therefore, was probably due at least in part to the financial support provided by Madison County settlers who, if not openly sympathetic with the defendants, at least wanted to do everything possible to help them escape legal repercussions.

Whoever they were, the sympathizers of the accused had assembled a team of seven defense attorneys who were the closest thing to hotshot legal troubleshooters available in central Indiana in 1824. The two lead attorneys, Fletcher and Martin M. Ray, were well-connected young go-getters at the start of celebrated careers that would within a few decades put them at the head of the state's legal establishment. Fletcher was a native Vermonter, twenty-six years of age, related by marriage to the great Daniel Webster. As a teenager he had worked his way on foot westward to Ohio, where he studied law in Urbana. When the Delaware resettlement opened central Indiana in 1821, Fletcher removed to the future capital of the new state, where he was admitted to the bar the next year before Wick and Judge Miles Eggleston, who would later preside over the trials of Sawyer and the Bridges.[17]

Ray, "a man of imposing appearance and high attainments" who arrived in Indianapolis as a trial lawyer from the southern Indiana town of Shelbyville, was already well-known and well-connected locally. His brother, James Brown Ray, became governor of the state while the Fall Creek trials were proceeding, and Martin Ray himself later directed one of the state capital's most distinguished and influential law firms, practicing for the next half century until killed by a sudden heart attack in 1872.[18]

While Ray and Fletcher were the strategists and orators who masterminded and presented the defense, their advisers who made up the rest of the defense team were just as high-powered. Bethuel F. Morris was an attorney and land agent at Indianapolis, soon to be a judge himself, who later founded the local "National Republican" Club and the Indiana Temperance Society. William Morris (Bethuel's brother), Lot Bloomfield, Charles H. Test, and James Rariden were all young frontier legal luminaries who later rose to prominence in the ranks of Hoosier lawyers and in the state government.

Johnston, caught off guard and taken aback by the unexpected arsenal of legal talent deployed for the defense, recognized a grave challenge to his

Calvin Fletcher in his later years. Fletcher was a young attorney at the beginning of his law career when he and Martin M. Ray headed the defense team.

and the federal government's hopes for a quick, successful prosecution. He doubted that the undistinguished team of local prosecuting attorneys, James Gilmore and Cyrus Ferich, were up to the task of parrying what he now anticipated would be a very skillfully conducted defense.[19] In a radical move, Johnston, with the support of the secretary of war, solicited James Noble, one of Indiana's U.S. senators, to act as special prosecutor—"counsel in aid of the prosecution," to use Johnston's term—in the case.[20]

The move was a shrewd one, and Johnston's choice could hardly have been better. Noble was one of the most popular politicians in the state and a part of what many described as the "ruling triumvirate" of Indiana politics, consisting of himself, Hendricks, and Jonathan Jennings, the state's first governor and leader of its democratic, anti-Harrison faction. The posts of governor, senator, and congressman circulated back and forth among these three, "changing hands as in a country dance."[21] They had worked together since the state's first constitutional convention in 1816 and selected the three judges who made up Indiana's first state supreme court bench. Born in Virginia around 1790, "General" Noble, as he was called from the days of the War of 1812, served as Indiana senator from the state's formation to his death in 1831. In that spring of 1824, he was arguably the best-known and most distinguished political figure in the state.[22]

Of particular importance to Johnston, who correctly anticipated an emotional trial, was Noble's standing as a renowned popular orator. While not particularly distinguished for his technical legal acumen, the senator was famed and feared as a peerless manipulator of jury sentiment. Johnston acknowledged all these considerations as factors influencing the selection of Noble, writing to McKenney that while Noble's "connection with the general government and his long and high standing as a public man in Indiana were the only inducements" for the senator's selection, Noble was also valuable for his "known zeal, industry and talents in working upon the feelings of a jury."[23]

Noble also had the good judgment to select two particularly able lieutenants, Harvey Gregg and Philip Sweetser, to assist with his prosecution. Gregg, a native Kentuckian with a reputation as a sharp-witted, "waggish lawyer," was the second attorney admitted to the bar in the city of Indianapolis. A leading literary light of the rude, future metropolis, he was famous as the founder of one of the city's newspapers, the *Western Censor and Emigrant's Guide*, and as possessor of its largest library, a collection that numbered more than 2,700 books when he arrived in 1821.[24] Sweetser, a young state's attorney from

Indianapolis, was on the threshold of a distinguished two-decade career in Indiana's Whig politics, a career no doubt forwarded by the fact that he was also Senator Noble's son-in-law.[25]

By the end of that spring of 1824 the main characters in the legal drama preparing to unfold in the valley of the White River had been cast. As far as concerns the professional arbiters of the law, both sides look very much alike. So much so, in fact, that it is hard to say what factors, besides the most obvious and mundane—the prospect for career advancement by involvement in a high-profile case and the natural desire for a hefty legal retainer—served to motivate the principals in either camp. Judges, prosecutors, and defenders were all part of one tight-knit band of local professionals, men adept at using their command of the law and the media to control the politics of the new state, while keeping a sharp eye on the main chance for promising investment in the region's newly opened and rapidly appreciating land.

Socially, all the principals in the trial of Hudson inhabited the same milieu of rambunctious, hard-drinking frontier literati. When not engaged in legal combat, for example, Judge Wick, defense attorney Bethuel Morris, and prosecutor Sweetser, opponents in the courtroom, were all united as brothers in the "Centre Lodge," the headquarters of Indianapolis Freemasonry.[26] Fletcher and Noble, soon to be jousting at the bar, were wealthy land speculators and good friends who carried on an amiable correspondence.[27] Politically, with Indiana still on the threshold of the dawning age of party politics, personal connections and a folksy touch with the electorate counted for more than abstract political principle and on the only issues that mattered—internal improvements and easy credit, an eternally appealing set of nonpartisan principles—prosecution, defense, and bench were united.

Nor were the parties to the trial divided by economic interest or status. They all shared a universal commitment to "progress" understood quite properly as appreciation of real estate values, and many on both sides were already heavily invested in New Purchase land, much of it in Madison County. Noble, Fletcher, Cory, Winchell, and Holliday, sympathizers of the accused such as Hiday, and supporters of the prosecution such as William Conner, were either already speculating in Madison County land or would do so during the course of the trial and in its immediate wake. Many, including Noble, Conner, Fletcher, and Ray, resided in other counties while eventually investing in hundreds of acres of Madison County real estate. Bethuel Morris had information before the move of the state capital from Corydon to Indianapolis and profited by the information, which he magnanimously shared with his crony Fletcher. Noble and Fletcher, for their parts, were unusually active speculators, appearing in numerous Madison County land transactions during the late 1820s and early 1830s.[28]

It is impossible to say whether the private feelings most of these men held toward the case and toward the accused differed from that implied in their professional roles as defenders and prosecutors. There is some evidence that Fletcher, a man already considered a paragon of integrity for his staunch commitment to the unpopular cause of abolition, was personally convinced of the guilt of the men he was defending. Working in the town of Rushville two weeks after the murders, Fletcher received a long letter from his wife, Sarah, writing from their Indianapolis home. Among the notes about health and household business, she remarks in passing that "B. F. has been up to be counsil for those men who committed the Indian murder." This must be a reference to defense attorney Bethuel F. Morris, and Sarah Fletcher's note conveys an unequivocal presumption of guilt.[29]

Whatever his personal opinions may have been, Fletcher set out with Ray to craft a determined defense of the accused when the circuit court commenced its fall session on Thursday, October 7. No courthouse yet existed, so the judges, the jury, the accused, and the spectators crammed into the one-room cabin of a Pendleton pioneer named William McCartney. Separated from the officials by a stout pole, a substantial crowd, including newspaper reporters and observers from as far away as Ohio, looked on at the free frontier drama about to be played out. Although Wick and his associates, for reasons not made clear in the transcripts, dismissed the original bills of indictment, new ones were quickly drawn up, and, on a motion of the defense, the court determined on separate trials for the prisoners. The prosecution moved to try Hudson first, on a charge set down by the court clerk in a labored legal prose that nonetheless conveys some sense of the moral outrage evoked by the crime:

> James Hudson and John Bridge late of said county labourers not having the fear of God before their eyes but being moved and seduced by the instigation of the Devil on the twentieth day of April . . . in and upon one Logan an Indian man in the peace of God and the state of Indiana then and there bring feloniously willfully and of their malice aforethought did make an assault . . . and kill and murder contrary to law and against the peace and dignity of the State of Indiana.[30]

The remainder of the first day of the court's session was spent in empanelling a petit jury to hear the charges against Hudson. Both foes and backers of
the accused attempted to pack the jury. Judge Winchell began the impropri-
eties, instructing the sheriff "to call Squire Makepeace on the jury, he is a good
man, and won't let a single murderer escape."[31]

Hudson's supporters were just as eager to corrupt the proceedings. When
Wick, as presiding judge, called for the bailiff to begin seating potential jurors,
Cory responded, "May it please the court, Dr. Highday [Hiday] just handed
me a list of jurors to call on the jury." Hiday, who Hudson believed was involved in a plan to poison Logan, was then questioned by Wick. "Dr. Highday,
is this your handwriting?" Upon Hiday's affirmative response, Wick expelled
the medical man from the proceedings, stating, "Dr. Highday, we have no jail
to put you in, the one we have is full. Hear your sentence, it is the judgment
of the court that you be banished from these court grounds till the trials are
over."[32]

Due to vigorous challenging by the defense attorneys, it was nearly
midnight before a jury was selected. Bethuel Morris was especially active in
suggesting that jurors could not be fairly selected because, as the transcripts
of the account put it, the juror believed "that the conviction and punishment
of the said defendant was necessary to secure himself, his family, and the
country from the retaliatory vengeance of the Indians."[33] Wick dismissed the
motion, and by the close of the day Hudson's jury of peers was complete.

Subsequent accounts make much of the rustic quality of the courtroom
population at Hudson's trial. Outsiders and memoirists enjoyed portraying
the picturesque antics of a pack of backwoods hayseeds. A visitor from Ohio
later reported finding Wick in the middle of the courtroom, "sitting on a block,
paring his nails." The jurors were customarily pictured as "heavy bearded" back-
woodsmen, hearing the case in their leather hunting suits, shod in moccasins,
knives thrust through their belts.[34]

These stories may be dismissed as historical embroidery that obscures
the reality of the shrewd men who oversaw and rendered a verdict in the trial.
Wick, an admittedly blunt character, was also a reflective and well-educated
man, as his emotional and learned closing oration in Hudson's trial made
abundantly evident. And the jurors were anything but a collection of colorful bumpkins, including among their number some of the more remarkable
citizens of the young state. John Marsh, for example, was already a prominent
local landowner who in coming years would take a leading role in local

Democratic politics. George Smith, another juror, had established the first
printing establishment in Indianapolis a few years earlier, was a prosperous
real estate agent, and later served as an associate judge.[35]

The trial proper began at 6 a.m. the following morning, when Sheriff Cory
escorted Hudson from the log stockade to the McCartney cabin. Six months in
the dirt-floored log cubicle by the falls had transformed Hudson. The powerful,
glowering brute remembered by Cox and Smith now seemed a physical wreck,
"pale, haggard and downcast," barely able to enter his plea of "not guilty" in
a broken voice.[36] The presentation of evidence took little time, amounting
almost to a mere formality. Only Andrew Jones appeared for the prosecution,
giving evidence in a brief testimony regarding the events, which Ray was unable to shake in cross-examination. The defense called no witnesses of its own.

Before noon, all the evidence had been presented, and both defense and
prosecution were prepared for their closing appeals to the jurors. Both sides
seemed convinced that the outcome of the trial would hinge less on weight
of evidence than on the emotional power of their final arguments. Ray, apparently desperate at his failure in cross-examination, based his hopes on a
straightforward appeal to naked racial hatred. He entirely ignored the evidence
against his client. Instead, he gambled on the power of a litany of a half-century's worth of Indian crimes against whites, "relating in glowing colors the
early massacres of white men, women and children, by the Indians; reading
the principal incidents in the history of Daniel Boone and Simon Kenton;
relating their cruelties at the battle of the Blue Licks and Bryant's Station, and
not forgetting the defeat of [Edward] Braddock, [Arthur] St. Clair and [Josiah]
Harmar."[37]

It was left to Noble to somehow counter the powerful appeal of racial
bigotry. He did so with a virtuosity that fully vindicated Johnston's determi-
nation that Noble was the man to lead the prosecution. His final declamation
against Hudson relied on two highly effective rhetorical tactics. Brandishing
the bloody clothes of the Indians before the seated jurors, the imposing senator on the one hand appealed to the natural sympathies and idealism of his
listeners. He reminded the jury of the humanity of Hudson's victims and of
their patriotic duty to uphold justice and the law. At the same time, he played
skillfully upon the fears of the frontiersmen, warning the jurors that their
safety and that of their families might depend upon the verdict since "the
chiefs and warriors expected justice to be done."[38]

Noble won. After being given a detailed charge by Wick, in which he elaborated upon the law of homicide and stressed that the law made no distinction between the killing of an Indian and a white, the jury took less than an hour to find Hudson "guilty in form and manner" of the charge against him. The defense was given until the following morning to prepare arguments against being given a sentence of death. Proceedings against Bridge, taken up after the rendering of Hudson's verdict, went long into the night, until they were stymied because, as Johnston put it, "twelve men could not be found who had not disqualified themselves in having expressed opinions unfavorable to the case of the prisoners."[39]

At sunrise on the morning of the ninth, the sheriff brought the convict Hudson once more before Wick, this time to hear his sentence. Wick opened by offering the defense an opportunity to show causes for "an arrest of judgment in the case," whereupon "the counsel for the accused then entered into elaborate discussions." Fletcher and Ray alleged five errors in the proceedings, which they claimed invalidated the trial and conviction. These centered largely upon matters of jury selection cited by Ray the day before and included such issues as the failure to permit Hudson himself to question potential jurors about whether fears of Indian vengeance would influence their judgment of the evidence.[40]

Ray's objections were not devoid of merit, but Wick impatiently dismissed them and prepared to pass sentence. In stately and measured tones, the judge briefly reviewed the case, praising the work of the defense team and approving the deliberations of the jury, which he said left "no grounds of a rational doubt in [Hudson's] favor." Wick then gave voice to an impassioned lament against the racial violence of the frontier in general, and against Hudson's crime in particular, noting the bitter irony that Logan came of a native people who deserved the gratitude of white Americans for their staunch support against the British during the last war. "How could you have the heart to make war upon, shoot, and destroy the venerable old chief, whose name ought to have been his passport from the Mississippi to the Atlantic?" he asked Hudson.[41]

Wick's rhetorical question was but the prelude to an extended and eloquent plea for justice for the natives, deriving both from the legitimate claims of history as well as Christian morality:

> O my God, how could you do it? How could you deprive your brother
> man of that life which was as dear to him as yours is to you? Logan,
> although an Indian, is a son of Adam, our common father. Then surely
> he was not the natural enemy of the white man. He was bone of your

James Noble's impassioned closing argument persuaded the jurors to convict James Hudson of murder.

bone, flesh of your flesh. Besides, by what authority do we hauntingly boast of our being white? What principle of philosophy or of religion establishes the doctrine that a white skin is preferable in nature or in the sight of God to a red or black one? Who has ordained that men of the white skin shall be at liberty to shoot and hunt down men of the red, or exercise rule and dominion over those of the black? The Indians of America have been more "sinned against than sinning." Our forefathers came across the broad Atlantic, and taking advantage of their fears and their simplicity obtained a resting place among the Indians, then the "lords of the soil," and since that time by a series of aggressions, have taken from them their homes and firesides—have pressed them westwardly until they were nearly extinct.[42]

Concluding this powerful apologia on behalf of justice for the red man, Wick lowered his voice and counseled Hudson that he must be prepared to meet his maker. Regretting that "it has for the first time in my life, become my duty to pronounce upon a fellow mortal the most awful sentence of the law," Wick delivered his sentence: "James Hudson the defendant be confined in close custody of the sheriff of Madison County in the common jail thereof from this time until Wednesday the first day of December next and that on the said Wednesday the first day of December next he the said James Hudson the defendant aforesaid be hanged by the neck until he be dead between the hours of ten o'clock in the forenoon and two o'clock in the afternoon."[43]

With a final "And a God of mercy have compassion on your soul," Wick thus confirmed the verdict and rendered the sentence sought by Johnston and his superiors. Johnston, however, could not yet breathe a sigh of relief, nor rest from his efforts on behalf of the prosecution. Anticipating an appeal, in the course of his sentencing, Wick also recommended that Governor Hendricks postpone the scheduled date of execution until the Indiana Supreme Court could either confirm or reverse the lower court's decision. In fact, Ray, Fletcher, and Hudson's other attorneys were preparing an elaborate appeal based upon their earlier objections that they planned to present at the supreme court's fall term in the second week of November.

In the meantime, Johnston was worried. Although the "vast crowds" who thronged the village of Pendleton to hear the trial and sentencing had behaved with "the greatest order and decorum," according to the local papers, Johnston detected a good deal of covert sympathy for the convict and his accomplices. The guards at the stockade near Pendleton struck him as lax, and Hendricks still dawdled in providing adequate support. "There being good grounds for the belief that an attempt would be made to rescue the prisoners on or before the time of Hudson's execution," he told McKenney, "after consulting General Noble and other persons obliged to confidence, the Governor of the State having neglected to order a force, I have employed a guard of ten men and an officer to command them . . . this force to continue employed until the prisoners are finally disposed of."[44]

His concern was well advised. In a unanimous decision issued on November 13, Justice Isaac Blackford, writing for the Indiana Supreme Court, rejected the motions of Hudson's attorneys and confirmed the trial verdict and sentence. Asking the potential jurors to admit prejudice, they declared, was tantamount to asking them to defame themselves, compelling the juror "to testify to his own depravity." The court could not admit this to be a legal principle. The validity of the circuit court trial was affirmed, and Hudson would be executed.[45]

The convict had other ideas. Two days after the supreme court's rejection of his appeal, on Saturday, November 15, Hudson escaped. His guards, possibly sympathizing with the condemned man or, as many said, believing him insane and harmless, permitted him to store bread and a pound and a half of dried beef under a broad belt. Hudson had long since learned to slip out of his now loose manacles. After the guard performed his evening check of the prisoners, at which he reported Hudson reading his Bible, the prisoner shed his manacles, got a fellow prisoner to boost him up the encircling palisade, and set out for freedom.

He did not get far. Fleeing the stockade, Hudson waded the frigid waters of Fall Creek heading northeast, toward the cover of the "Prairie Swamp" and the eventual destination of Fort Wayne, making in fact for the very site of the murders, but Fall Creek proved his undoing. Soaked and chilled to the bone, with frozen feet, the escapee crept into a hollow log no more than a quarter mile from his prison. He cowered there with no fire through two days of cold and steady drizzle, as frostbite slowly numbed his feet, emerging on Monday to stumble some six or seven miles farther upstream. There he sought shelter under the floorboards of an abandoned cabin. The condition of his feet worsened, and though tempted to steal a horse, he claimed his conscience would not permit the theft. "Providence acted against my design."

Feverish and sick, Hudson hid beneath the cabin until Tuesday the twenty-fifth. Eventually tortured by thirst, he finally emerged from his lair to drink water from the nearby creek, where he collapsed on its bank, racked by tremors and vomiting. Either delirious or aware of his dire condition and recognizing his desperate need for help, Hudson hailed a passing farmer named Penn, who helped the prisoner to his nearby cabin. Cory had posted a reward of one hundred dollars for the escapee, and the case was a cause célèbre. Penn would have had little doubt about the identity of the helpless unfortunate in his cabin. After removing Hudson's moccasins to tend his damaged feet, the farmer notified Cory, and Hudson returned under guard to his cell back at Pendleton.[46]

He had six weeks to live, since Hendricks had granted a delay of execution during the period of Hudson's flight. As he awaited the new date, January 12, 1825, Hudson passed his time praying, reading the Bible, dictating his dramatic "Confession" to Indianapolis reporter Samuel Woodworth, and talking with pastor Benjamin Miller. Friends of the condemned farmer failed in a final appeal for a pardon from Hendricks.[47] A last letter from his wife, Phebe, who had returned to her family in Preble County, Ohio, promised him in moving terms that "Nothing, nor no circumstance, that ever has happened, has ever turned my affections from you . . . and if we never meet on earth, I trust to meet you in Heaven, where parting will be no more."[48] Meanwhile, across Fall Creek, a gallows was being built at the base of a small hill about one hundred feet north of the falls.

Hudson's coffin, originally constructed to be ready for his December execution date, had been his companion at the jail since his recapture, a constant, silent reminder of his impending fate. On the morning of the twelfth, the military guard placed the wooden box in a wagon, hoisted the crippled Hudson—hands bound at his back, round his neck the hangman's rope—to a seat atop it, and set out for the bottomland on the north bank of Fall Creek.

A small, curving hill rises to the northeast of the site, forming a hollow around the low-lying edge of the creek bed. Now, this natural amphitheater was dark with the crowd of spectators who had flocked from all over the Indiana frontier and beyond to watch the curtain fall on Hudson's part in the frontier tragedy. A number of Indians, said to be Seneca and Shawnee, stood on the hill apart from the whites, some hundred or so yards from the gallows.

When the wagon bearing the condemned prisoner arrived at the gallows, Miller read from the Gospel of Matthew—admonishing the culprit and his hearers to follow the example of the wise virgins. Afterwards, as the prisoner

The falls of Fall Creek as they appear today. The executions took place on the right banks of the falls and the criminals allegedly were buried in the village cemetery two hundred yards north of this place.

was helped onto the scaffold, supported over the trap by two guards, Thomas Pendleton read a final prayer. In tears, praising God for his goodness, Hudson admitted his deed, saying he had been misled into murder by associates. With his last request, he begged for a proper burial. His guards stepped aside. The trapdoor swung, and Hudson plunged to his reward.[49]

"We Are Satisfied": A Family on the Gallows

For thirty-five minutes, the murderer's body hung before the silent and slowly dispersing crowd. Logan was avenged, before all the world. Following the corpse's public display, the militia cut it down and prepared it for burial. A day later Hudson was interred in what would eventually grow into the village cemetery north of the falls. Johnston must have been gratified. The conclusion to the first of the trials, from the point of view of the Indian Affairs bureaucracy, could hardly have been more satisfactory. But, Johnston's work was far from finished. Three prisoners—Bridge Sr., his son, and his wife's brother,

Andrew Sawyer—still awaited the spring term of the Madison County Circuit Court, scheduled to begin in May.

The long wait was beginning to fray the nerves of the accused. Come May, they would have spent more than a year festering in their dank log hut. The tension and deprivation nearly exploded into further killing even before Hudson's execution. While waiting for the Indiana Supreme Court to respond to Hudson's appeal in October, Bridge Jr. broke down, telling the guards that his father and uncle had forced him to help kill Logan. This betrayal was too much for the older man. Enraged by this further evidence of the boy's shaky nerves, the two older men attacked the teenager, nearly throttling him before the guards intervened.[50]

After Hudson's execution, during the winter and spring of 1825, the prisoners continued to mark time, apparently without incident. Outside their palisaded world, however, important changes transformed the legal landscape. In response to Indiana's continued growth, the state legislature modified and expanded the court system. Madison County was attached to the Third Circuit, rather than the Fifth Circuit. A new presiding judge, Miles Eggleston, took Wick's place when the trials resumed in May. In addition, thanks to complaints that had come from Johnston, the governor, and many legal professionals, the legislature extended the permissible length of the circuit court session. To Johnston's relief, there would be no more frustrating deadlines to extend the case beyond the spring session.

New faces also assumed the lead roles when the Fall Creek drama resumed. Oliver H. Smith was the chief prosecutor for the Third Circuit, and he was not a man to stand aside and let others dominate such a celebrated case. The self-taught attorney had started his career as a teen, reading for two years, answering a few questions put by a circuit judge, and gaining his license. He quickly gained fame on the Hoosier trial circuit. A tireless traveler and popular, backslapping good old boy, he was later recalled as "a fine specimen of the shrewd, genial, dry-witted, horse-trading Hoosier public man of no more than ordinary ability, a type that persists to this day."[51]

A cheerful cynic, Smith candidly admitted his own shortcomings in describing his first congressional campaign in 1825, not coincidentally the very year he earned statewide renown for his role at Fall Creek, "Stump speaking was just coming into fashion and the people flocked to hear us by the thousands. My opponent had a good knowledge of the issues and I had a powerful voice."[52] The voters chose Smith. Then, as now, the sky was the limit to what such an endearing scoundrel could do politically, and Smith's candor eventually earned him a place in the Senate. He was too shrewd not to recognize a golden opportunity in the sensational cases in Madison County, and though Noble remained on the team, Smith quickly became the voice of the prosecution.

Facing Smith, a new adversary was preparing to take the lead for the defense. While Fletcher, Ray, and the Morrises remained with the defense team, the young Rariden guided the fight to acquit Sawyer and the two Bridges. An intense, determined character who boasted no formal education, Rariden acquired his taste for law while working in the Indiana town of Salisbury as the assistant to the clerk of Wayne County. Despite a sinister aspect—the short, barrel-chested Rariden had a head of thick black hair, piercing black eyes, and a withered left arm that he carried in a sling—he was famed as an eloquent speaker who easily reduced juries to tears and as a devastating tactician in cross-examination.

Rariden's tenacity of character was legendary. Despite the use of only one arm, he had worked for years in his youth as a manual laborer and was said to have split hundreds of rails in a single day. In 1825 Rariden was also on the brink of a long career in Indiana politics that saw see him elected to the U.S. Congress and to the Indiana Constitutional Convention of 1851. Unlike his fellow defender, Fletcher, he opposed the extension of rights to blacks on the basis of a "higher law" of white racial supremacy.[53]

With Eggleston presiding, and Holliday and Winchell again serving as associates, proceedings in the case resumed on Monday, March 9. The entire first day of the session was taken up in empanelling a grand jury and producing new indictments. Consulting Johnston and Noble, Smith elected to prosecute Sawyer first, for the shooting of one of the Indian women at the camp. On the next morning, a petit jury was quickly selected, the process having been simplified since the preceding session "under a late decision of our Supreme Court, that a juror, in a criminal case, shall not be asked if has *formed* or *expressed* an opinion as to the guilt or innocence of the *accused*."[54]

The trial, like Hudson's, took very little time. The presentation of evidence—there is no preserved record as to its nature, which presumably involved the testimony of prosecution witnesses Jones and Sawyer—occupied only part of the morning. Rariden and Bethuel Morris then spoke for the prisoner, with Noble closing in another "powerful speech" for the State.[55] Although the surviving sources are maddeningly vague, it is clear that for some reason Noble was less effective now than he had been the previous fall. After listening to the attorneys, the jury retired for fifteen hours. It was not until 10 o'clock on the following morning that they were able to return with a verdict. The jury found Sawyer guilty, of manslaughter, not murder, because he had "acted under mental excitement and rage in the horrid tragedy."[56] He was to serve two years in prison and pay a fine of one hundred dollars.

This was a defeat for Johnston and the State. Why were the Madison County jurors, who had quickly decided that Hudson was guilty of murder, inclined to greater leniency in Sawyer's killing of the Indian woman? Conceivably the evident misery of the prisoner—"he appeared so haggard and changed by his long confinement, that I hardly knew him"—elicited some sympathy, but Hudson had also been a clearly broken man at the time of his trial.[57] Other accounts also noted the impact of Sawyer's changed appearance, "The long imprisonment had left him haggard and weak, exciting a feeling of pity among the onlookers."[58] It is also possible that Hudson's ambush of the stately and well-respected Logan evoked greater outrage in Hudson's jurors than did Sawyer's murder, which was perpetrated later in that day upon a nameless and unknown Indian woman, and only after the bloodletting had already been initiated.

The events that followed Sawyer's verdict and sentencing are confused. According to Smith, writing nearly forty years later, Rariden immediately sprang to his feet, calling for the next case against Sawyer to be heard, using the same jury that had just returned the verdict.[59] Contemporary newspaper accounts, as well as subsequent histories of Madison County, tell a different story, in which the remainder of Wednesday was taken up with the trial of John Bridge Jr. This seems more likely. While it is true that the lists of jurors in the trials of the three men during that week in May show the recurrence of many of the same names on successive juries, it is not likely that a jury returned from fifteen hours of deliberation would be immediately reseated for a new case. Nor is it probable that a shrewd team of prosecutors would agree to proceed with a jury that had shown such sympathy to the defendant. As has been seen, Smith appears to have enjoyed a colorful story without regard for its complete accuracy. The reliability of the contemporary newspapers and local histories is probably to be preferred.

Bridge Jr. faced two murder charges, one for twice driving his hunting knife through Logan's chest, and the other for aiding Hudson in the killing of the same person by shooting. Bridge Jr., therefore, was being tried on two murder charges in the death of the same individual. For all their acumen, none of his attorneys seemed to raise this as an issue with the court. Although Bridge Jr. denied both counts, the evidence was quickly reviewed, and after three hours a verdict of guilty on both counts was returned.

But Bridge's youth and demeanor worked in his favor. "The age of young Bridge, together with his known penitence since his confinement, excited much sympathy—notwithstanding the second count indictment was proved beyond a doubt," the *Indianapolis Journal* reported.[60] The jury was sensitive to these facts, and the foreman concluded his reading of the verdict by expressing the belief of his fellows "that the defendant was proper object of executive mercy, and seriously urge pardon."[61]

The next day Bridge Sr. was tried on counts of murdering and assisting in the murder of the women and children at the camp. He seemed to have weathered his confinement better than the younger men. "He was more firm in his step, and looked better than Sawyer, though a much older man," Smith later claimed.[62] The outcome, however, was no different. The evidence presented in his case—"practically a repetition of that offered in the others"—was sufficiently persuasive that the jury took only minutes to return a verdict of guilty.[63] One of the most damning elements of the case against Bridge Sr. was the commission of an act that others had attributed to Sawyer, "It was proved that the defendant [Bridge Sr.] took an Indian boy, of the age of three or four years, by the heels and dashed his brains out against a beech tree."[64]

On the following morning, appropriately Friday the thirteenth, Sawyer was again tried. Here, too, accounts vary. Histories written later declare that Sawyer was also indicted for the murder of an Indian boy. Noble, according to these accounts, made a passionate plea, once again waving the bloody clothes of the victim before the men of the jury and bringing them to tears. Smith closed with an elaborate oration on the moral distinction between the murder of a full-grown woman and a small child.[65]

Smith remembered it differently. Attributing to himself Noble's tactic with the bloody shirt, he later recalled delivering a devastatingly persuasive oration to the jury:

> And holding it up to the jury "Yes, gentlemen of the jury, the cases are very different. You might find the prisoner guilty of only man-slaughter in using his rifle on a grown squaw; that was the work of a man, but this was the work of a demon. Look at this shirt, gentlemen, with the bloody stains upon it; this was a poor helpless boy, who was taken

by the heels by this fiend in human shape, and his brains knocked
out against a log! If the other case was man-slaughter, was not this
murder?"[66]

Contemporaries at the time, however, recorded none of this. In fact,
Sawyer appears to have been tried on Friday for the murder of Ludlow in the
woods, not for killing any of the victims at the camp. Rariden in defense par-
ried cleverly, urging leniency and arguing that the community was prejudiced
against the accused by its fear of a retaliatory Indian uprising, certainly a
plausible assertion. Valid or not, the defense plea did no good. It took the jury
only minutes to find Sawyer guilty of murder, as charged.[67]

With all three of the accused now convicted, Eggleston summoned them
after the reading of Sawyer's second verdict to hear their sentencing. Accounts
written at the time describe Sawyer and the elder Bridge, brought before the
judge, attempting to minimize their crimes. Allegedly, Sawyer had even been
seen to smile and laugh during the earlier proceedings. Others, including
Smith, recount a much more dramatic, and perhaps predictable, moment:

> The prisoners rose, tears streaming down their faces, and their groans
> and sighs filled the courtroom. I fixed my eyes upon Judge Eggleston.
> I had heard him pronounce sentence of death upon Fuller, for the
> murder of Warren, and upon Fields for the murder of Murphy. But
> here was a still more solemn scene. An aged father, his favorite son,
> and his wife's brother—all standing before him to receive sentence
> of death.[68]

Eggleston did not flinch. All three men, not excepting young Bridge, were to
be hanged in three weeks, on June 3, between the hours of 10 o'clock in the
morning and five o'clock in the afternoon.

There was a chance, however, that the judge's sentence might not be
carried out. No evidence exists that an effort was made to gain a reversal, or
even to file an appeal, on behalf of Sawyer and Bridge Sr. But Bridge Jr., whose
emotional behavior at the proceedings had evoked a great deal of popular
sympathy, managed to persuade the court to recommend a pardon by the governor, now James Brown Ray, the brother of his defense attorney, Martin M.
Ray. Despite the appalling brutality of his behavior on the day of the killings,
locals began to circulate a petition for clemency. Bridge Jr., the petitioners
argued, "from his youth, ignorance, and the manner in which he was led into
the transaction, he being a lad only of the age of seventeen years at the time

the unhappy murder was committed," should be granted "a complete pardon of the crime and punishment aforesaid."[69]

The petition ultimately collected ninety-four signatures, a number equal to nearly 15 percent of Madison County's white population. While the sheer quantity of residents willing to thus go on record in support of a convicted killer is remarkable in itself, the nature of the men who called for clemency (and the list of signatories is of course 100 percent male) is even more noteworthy. They comprise a veritable roll call of central Indiana's pioneer elite. Included among those calling for mercy were Sawyer's old adversary Conrad Crosley, "Squire" Makepeace, David Ellsworth, and others who had just served as jurors at the trials; influential defense attorneys Martin Ray and William Morris; Miller, the county's most prominent churchman; William Conner, perhaps the wealthiest capitalist on the Indiana frontier; Thomas H. Pendleton, who would found the town at the falls named for him; Doctor Hiday, whom Hudson notoriously charged with providing poison; Samuel Woodworth, journalist and ghostwriter for Hudson's "Confession"; Moses Cox; William McCartney, whose cabin had housed the court; and many more.

The petition was the only attempt to avert the fate awaiting the convicts, and by the execution date, June 3, 1825, Governor Ray had not responded. On the morning of the third, accordingly, Cory escorted Sawyer and Bridge Sr. to the site of execution at the hill by the falls. An execution was always a gratifying spectacle, and one in such a sensational case—a triple hanging, no less—drew large crowds. Thousands turned out this fine June morning, among them a number of Seneca Indian chiefs brought from Ohio at government expense (and against their will, according to John Johnston).[70] Those hoping for an exciting show would not be disappointed.

If a scaffold or gallows was ever actually constructed for the execution of Hudson, it seems to have disappeared by this time, five months later. Instead, the bed of the wagon in which the prisoners were transported became their gallows. As they approached the hill, the Reverend John Strange, a famous frontier Methodist preacher who appears to have usurped the role of local favorite Miller, sermonized. The wagon stopped, and Cory told the condemned men that they had but few moments left, and if they wished to make a last statement, they would have to do it now.

"Bridge arose and reported that he had made a confession in writing, and that it would shortly be published," eyewitnesses wrote, "and therefore he considered it unnecessary to recapitulate it; but said he was *in part* guilty of the crime for which he was about to suffer. He admonished the spectators, particularly the young people, to take warning by his untimely end, and flee from the wrath to come—Sawyer said but little. In a few minutes after they were launched into eternity."[71]

A ghastly misstep, however, intervened briefly to keep Sawyer from his fate. John H. B. Nowland was an early chronicler of Indiana history, who was also an eyewitness in the crowd at the falls that morning:

> A wagon was drawn up on the side of the hill, with the wheels on planks, so they would move easy and quickly, a post was placed on the side of the hill just above the wagon; to this post the wagon was fastened by a rope, so that when the rope was cut the wagon would run down the hill without aid. The two old men were placed in the tail of the wagon, the ropes adjusted, the white caps drawn over their faces and at a given signal the rope was cut and wagon quickly run from under the unfortunate men. [72]

Such a makeshift gallows, however, failed to generate sufficient force to break the neck of a strong man such as Sawyer. "He broke his arms loose that were pinioned behind," Nowland writes, "he caught the rope by which he was hanging and raised himself about eighteen inches; the sheriff [Cory] quickly caught him by the ankles, gave a sudden jerk, which brought the body down, and he died without another struggle."[73]

The dead men hung for thirty minutes. Then, the sheriff and his deputies cut down the corpses and placed them in their coffins. Reluctantly, Cory returned to the jail to bring back Bridge Jr. Waiting until the last moment, hoping for the appearance of Governor Ray or for a pardon, Strange again addressed the condemned man and the crowd. At last, with the assistance of the sheriff, the young man stood up in the wagon. Before the hood could be drawn over his head, glancing at the bodies of his father and his uncle, he appeared to some observers to be in the process of losing his reason.

At this moment the crowd around the wagon track parted with a murmur, while a figure on horseback dashed down through the throng. This, at last, was Indiana's new governor: "All eyes saw Governor J. Brown Ray galloping majestically down in the direction of the gallows. He was mounted upon a superb horse, splendidly caparisoned, and was himself dressed in the finest attire. His face wore a look of supreme self-importance."[74] Ray, "perhaps the most eccentric man ever to be elected to the highest office in Indiana," was also renowned

Governor James Brown Ray's last-minute dramatic pardon saved John Bridge Jr.

for his colossal vanity, a reputation that he confirmed by becoming the first ever to put himself forward as a candidate for governor.[75]

Tossing the reins to a bystander, Brown strode toward the gallows.

"Young man," he asked Bridge, "do you know who stands before you?"

"No sir."

"Well, then it is time that you should know. There are sir, but two beings in this great universe who can save you from death; one is the great God of Heaven, and the other is James Brown Ray, governor of Indiana, who now stands before you. Here is your pardon. Go, sir, and sin no more!"[76]

Ray, God's coequal, had performed this trick before, pardoning an aged Revolutionary War veteran on the gallows. No one at the falls felt inclined to be cynical at the time, however. Ignoring the governor's repellent exhibitionism, and the brutal sadism he showed in delaying the pardon to this moment, the crowd broke into cheers. If he sought to win plaudits, Ray succeeded. "The governor in exercising this high authority of the constitution," wrote the *Indianapolis Gazette*, "has acted in accordance with the wishes not only of the jury and officers of the court who tried young Bridge, but of most of the citizens of the state."[77]

More importantly, perhaps, both Johnston and his Indian observers believed that the affair had come to an appropriate conclusion. Privately, Johnston had favored the clemency appeal on behalf of Bridge Jr., on grounds of his youth and because "his life appears to be necessary for the support of his mother."[78] The Seneca chiefs felt the same. Retribution, perhaps, was in fact less satisfying to them than many whites believed. They appeared to approve of the pardon of Bridge Jr., and they were clearly distressed by the hangings of Sawyer and Bridge Sr. "As an instance that Indians do not always look upon the death of those who have injured them with perfect indifference, it has been remarked that during the hangings they shed tears." Questioned by Johnston in the aftermath of the executions, the leader of the Seneca passed judgment for his people: "We are satisfied."[79]

Aftermath

The Great Cave of Memory

"The great cave of memory, and I know not what hidden and inexpressible recesses within it, takes in all these things to be called up and brought forth when there is need for them. All these enter in, each by its own gateway, and are laid away within it."[1]

AUGUSTINE

Governor James Brown Ray's theatrical pardon of John Bridge Jr. ended the episode known as the Fall Creek Massacre. The furor died out even more rapidly than it had blown up in the previous spring. The national spotlight that shone briefly on the little village at the falls of Fall Creek faded and never returned. With the play over, the characters left the stage. John Johnston, the impresario whose behind-the-scenes activity drove the entire affair, watched the hangings and then departed Madison County by night, traveling east across country under cover of darkness in fear that friends of the dead men might do him mischief. At Greenville, Ohio, he attached himself for protection to a traveling circus, in whose company he reached his home at Piqua. If he saw any irony in leaving Fall Creek in such company, he never indicated it.[2]

Though the murders, trials, and executions soon disappeared from all but local memories, they provided a helpful boost to the careers of many of those involved. For Oliver H. Smith, Fall Creek was remembered as "his most celebrated prosecution."[3] Later in 1825, the notoriety he gained through his involvement in the events at Madison County helped Smith to win his first campaign for Congress, starting him on the road that eventually led to the Senate and his role decades later as a kind of elder statesman of Indiana politics. Ray also made hay from Fall Creek. He had become governor in 1825 when William Hendricks resigned to take a seat in Congress. In the same week that he galloped up brandishing his popular pardon of John Bridge Jr., Ray brazenly put himself forward as a candidate for the post in the elections of 1825.[4] He won. Three years later he was reelected to a second term. Most of the young attorneys who had participated in the trials, whether for the prosecution or the defense, also prospered. Philip Sweetser, Harvey Gregg, Calvin

Fletcher, James Rariden, and Bethuel F. Morris all grew rich and powerful in the years following the trials. While still in their infancy, the careers of many of the men who dominated Indiana politics for decades crossed paths at McCartney's log cabin courthouse.

The surviving perpetrators, so far as can be known, also seem to have gotten along fairly well after the excitement of 1825 died down. Excluding the mysterious Thomas Harper, three of the gang who butchered Logan's people the previous March—Stephen Sawyer, Andrew Jones, and Bridge Jr.—remained alive when the executions concluded in June of 1825. All were young men who might have been expected to have long lives ahead of them, but nothing has been recorded of the fates of the two state witnesses, Sawyer and Jones. For decades after the killings, a host of contradictory rumors circulated around Bridge Jr. According to some, he died of a broken heart shortly after his pardon. Others insisted that he lost his reason and died in an asylum a year after the trials. Still others claimed, with a good deal of plausibility, that he vanished into the western wilderness.

In fact, Bridge Jr. lived in or near Indiana for another half century. After his harrowing moment on the scaffold, he returned to Butler County, Ohio, with members of his family, working for many years as a farm laborer. In 1834 he took a wife, settled in Carroll County, Indiana, and prospered as a dry goods merchant. As an old man in the year 1872, Bridge returned to the falls for a view of the site of the searing events—land that had become a part of the town founded after his pardon by petitioner Thomas Pendleton. Four years later Bridge died peacefully at Delphi, Indiana.[5]

For the U.S. government and its servants the case turned out about as well as could have been hoped. Johnston had shown great skill in managing the cooperation of federal and local authorities, and in using federal resources—at an ultimate cost of perhaps seven thousand dollars—to assuage the feelings of local Indians. By his efforts, he prevented the killings from causing any of the disruptions that were feared, and the removal of native tribes from Ohio, the Great Lakes, and the entire region east of the Mississippi continued.[6] Neither the settlement and development of the New Purchase, nor the steady appreciation in the value of its land, were slowed by the settler rampage in the valley of the White River. The only real losers from the point of view of the white community were three brutal and hapless farmers. Compared to the financial and human costs of a frontier war, the government got off with a bargain.

The events at Fall Creek, ironically, probably mattered least for those very tribal peoples in whose defense Johnston, Thomas L. McKenney, and the U.S. government claimed to be acting. Despite the sincere commitment of many in the Indian Affairs bureaucracy to the ideal of equal protection for red and white, the guilty verdict of the white jury in Madison County remained an extreme abnormality, the almost unique consequence of the perfect combination, in one place and one time, of specific personalities and specific conditions. Again and again in the following decades, individual white men and white mobs acted with impunity in wreaking bloody mayhem upon peaceful Indians—notoriously at sites such as Sand Creek and Camp Grant, as well as in countless other remembered incidents. The impartial justice toward which Johnston labored in 1824 and 1825 remained unrealized.[7]

To later generations, in times shaken once more by massive migrations and interethnic bloodshed, the legacy of the events at Fall Creek remains ambiguous. Inspiration may certainly be taken from some aspects of the episode. The fact that men such as Judge William Wick, Senator James Noble, and Smith could successfully appeal to a sense of the common humanity of

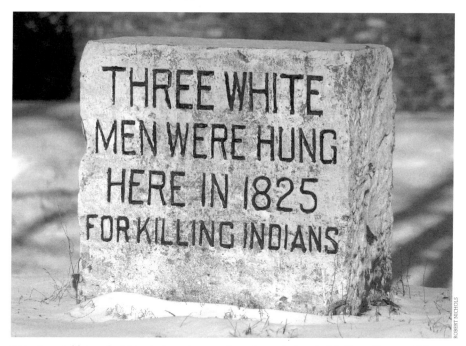

This stone tablet and a historical marker are the only reminders in Madison County of the Fall Creek Massacre.

the dead Indians to their audience of white jurors, members of a community in which hatred of the Indians was widespread and widely accepted, could be taken as a heartening instance of the triumph of human brotherhood over racial allegiance. Less inspiring, though, is the fact that the broader community of American whites found it convenient to gradually forget the episode. As a nation, Americans chose to let the example of Fall Creek remain an anomaly.

Its standing as a symbol of unrealized ideals, however, is not the only reason for the gradual disappearance of the Fall Creek Massacre from general memory. The frustrating murk of inaccuracy and fable that surrounds nearly all the most basic facts, typified by the popular mythology about the fate of Bridge Jr., has certainly helped to thwart historical memory. The flawed and partial record keeping of a turbulent frontier community, faulty recollection, garbled and incomplete redactions by observers, courthouse fires, all the blemishes that mar and gradually efface the historical record, play a role here. Even the records of Grove Lawn cemetery at Pendleton, presumably the "village burial ground" that holds the graves of James Hudson, John T. Bridge Sr., and Andrew Sawyer, were destroyed by fire.

Memory is a persistent thing, though. What is laid up in its "great cave," to take Augustine's image, endures. Perhaps without knowing why, and certainly without knowing their ultimate purpose, communities sometimes seem, without much deliberate intent or volition, to preserve the most vital parts of their shared past. Fall Creek, quickly forgotten by the nation at large, did not die out altogether or go away. It has hung on, a persistent presence in the group memory of its locale. Stored, in a sense, for a time when it would be more relevant to a people whose commitment to equal justice required such memories, it lay waiting "to be called up and brought forth when there is need."

Notes

Introduction

1. Thucydides, *The Peloponnesian War* (Chicago: Encyclopedia Britannica, 1952), 354.

2. The definitive work on relations between the U.S. government and the Indians, Francis Paul Prucha, *The Great Father: The United States Government and the American Indians* (Lincoln: University of Nebraska Press, 1984), and most standard works of the era say nothing about Fall Creek. The same applies to more recent standard works, including R. Douglas Hurt, *The Indian Frontier, 1763–1846* (Albuquerque: University of New Mexico Press, 2002); Paula Mitchell Marks, *In a Barren Land: The American Indian and the Quest for Cultural Survival, 1607 to the Present* (New York: Harper-Perennial, 1999); Jake Page, *In the Hands of the Great Spirit: The 20,000-Year History of American Indians* (New York: Simon and Schuster, 2003); Roger L. Nichols, *Indians in the United States and Canada: A Comparative History* (Lincoln: University of Nebraska Press, 1998); Bruce G. Trigger and Wilcomb E. Washburn, eds., *The Cambridge History of the Native People of the Americas*, vol. 1, *North America*, pt. 1 (Cambridge: Cambridge University Press, 1996). Where noted, the incident is typically mentioned only in passing, as in William M. Osborn, *The Wild Frontier: Atrocities during the American-Indian War from Jamestown Colony to Wounded Knee* (New York: Random House, 2000), 166; Stewart Rafert, *The Miami Indians of Indiana: A Persistent People, 1654–1994* (Indianapolis: Indiana Historical Society, 1996), or Herman J. Viola, *Thomas L. McKenney: Architect of America's Early Indian Policy, 1816–1830* (Chicago: Sage Books, 1974), 183.

3. Carl Waldman, ed., *Who Was Who in Native American History* (New York: Facts on File, 1990), vi. Or, as Larry McMurtry has put it, other than the fact that "a lot of people turned up dead," "all other statements need to be regarded with caution." Larry McMurtry, *Oh What a Slaughter: Massacres in the American West, 1846–1890* (New York: Simon and Schuster, 2005), 164. McMurtry also comments at some length on the Fall Creek Massacre, noting specifically the paucity of reliable sources.

4. Trial transcript, *State of Indiana v. John Bridge and James Hudson*, Fifth Judicial Circuit, October Session 1824, enclosed in appeal of attorneys Martin M. Ray and Calvin Fletcher to Indiana Supreme Court, November Term, 1824, pp. 5, 6 (Archives Division, Indiana Commission on Public Records, Indianapolis). The disregard for detail was not atypical. Cox "could barely write his name," according to the county prosecutor O. H. Smith. Cox also neglected to record the verdict in the first trial ever conducted in the county, a slander case brought by Conrad Crossly against Andrew Sawyer, whose paths crossed again in the aftermath of Sawyer's participation in the murders. See O. H. Smith, *Early Indiana Trials and Sketches* (Cincinnati: Moore, Wilstach, Keys and Company, 1858), 53, and T. B. Helm, ed., *History of Madison County, Indiana, with Illustrations and Biographical Sketches of Some of Its Prominent Men and Pioneers* (Chicago: Kingman Brothers, 1880), 28.

5. Cass commented on the killings in an essay written for the *North American Review*, which is reproduced in W. L. G. Smith, *Fifty Years of Public Life: The Life and Times of Lewis Cass* (New York: Derby and Jackson, 1856), 159.

Chapter 1

1. Joseph Conrad, *Under Western Eyes* (New York: Random House, 2001), xxi.

2. As already noted, key sources differ on a number of significant details, such as the exact

composition of the party of murderers, the tribal identity of the Indians, and the makeup of the Indian band. These discrepancies will be dealt with at greater length in the account of the apprehension and trial of the killers. For now, this account of the murders is based upon a synthesis of the most compatible evidence drawn from the following sources: *Pendleton Daily Register*, July 7, 1876; *Washington (NY) Republican and Congressional Examiner*, April 19, 1824; George Chalou, "Massacre on Fall Creek," *Prologue: The Journal of the National Archives* 4 (Summer 1972): 109–14; Sandford C. Cox, *Recollections of the Early Settlement of the Wabash Valley* (Lafayette, IN: Courier Steam, 1860), 9–12; Brian M. Doerr, "The Massacre at Deer Lick Creek, Madison County, Indiana, 1824," *Indiana Magazine of History* 93 (March 1997): 19–47; John L. Forkner, *History of Madison County, Indiana: A Narrative Account of Its Historical Progress, Its People, and Its Principal Interests* (Chicago: Lewis Publishing, 1914), 312–13; Samuel Woodworth, *Life and Confession of James Hudson, Who Was Executed on Wednesday the 12th January, 1825, at the Falls of Fall Creek for the Murder of Logan, an Indian Chief of the Wyandott Nation* (Indianapolis: Printed at the Gazette Office for the author, 1825), passim.; Leonard U. Hill, ed., *John Johnston and the Indians in the Land of the Three Miamis* (Piqua, 1957), 162–65; J. J. Netterville, ed., *Centennial History of Madison County Indiana: An Account of One Hundred Years of Progress, 1823–1923*, 2 vols. (Anderson, IN: Historians' Association Publishers, 1925), 1:70–80; John H. B. Nowland, *Early Reminiscences of Indianapolis, with Short Biographical Sketches of Its Early Citizens, and a Few of the Prominent Business Men of the Present Day* (Indianapolis: Sentinel, 1870), 164–66; *Anderson Democrat*, May 1, 1874; O. H. Smith, *Early Indiana Trials and Sketches* (Cincinnati: Moore, Wilstach, Keys and Company, 1858), 51–57, 176–79; and Trial transcript, *State of Indiana v. John Bridge and James Hudson*, Fifth Judicial Circuit, October Session 1824, enclosed in appeal of attorneys Martin M. Ray and Calvin Fletcher to Indiana Supreme Court, November Term, 1824 (Archives Division, Indiana Commission on Public Records, Indianapolis).

3. For a detailed discussion of the origins, specifications, capabilities, and ubiquity of this weapon in the early nineteenth century, see Charles Edward Chapel, *Guns of the Old West: An Illustrated Guide* (1961; reprint, Mineola, NY: Dover Publications, 2002), 19–22.

4. See, for example, Hill, ed., *John Johnston and the Indians in the Land of the Three Miamis*, 162, and Netterville, ed., *Centennial History of Madison County Indiana*, 1:71.

5. Woodworth, *Life and Confession of James Hudson*, 4, 5.

6. Ibid., 11.

7. On land prices, see *Pendleton Times*, June 2, 1949. A useful guide to the sorts of edged weapons that Ludlow and Logan might have carried is Colin F. Taylor, *Native American Weapons* (Norman: University of Oklahoma Press, 2001).

8. More than a century later, locals still remembered the Lick as "a deerhunter's paradise." See Raymond Davis, *Etcetera* (Evansville, IN: Unigraphic, 1971), 86.

9. Woodworth, *Life and Confession of James Hudson*, 13–14.

10. Ibid., 15. Cox, *Recollections of the Early Settlement of the Wabash Valley*, describes the site where the bodies were deposited variously as a "sink-hole" and a "clay-hole." It is now a dry pond.

Chapter 2

1. Alexis de Tocqueville, *Democracy in America*, Henry Reeve, trans., 2 vols. (New Rochelle, NY: Arlington House, n.d.), 1:331.

2. John Tipton, Indian agent at Fort Wayne in northern Indiana, estimated in 1824 that there were 2,441 Indians under his agency. Dorothy Riker and Nellie Armstrong Robertson, eds., *The John Tipton Papers*, 3 vols. (Indianapolis: Indiana Historical Bureau, 1942), 1:408. John

Johnston, the Indian agent for the Delaware and other nearby tribes, estimated that the Indians remaining in the state could assemble as many as 1,000 warriors, implying a total population some times that size. As late as 1828 the missionary Timothy Flint believed that the Indians in northern Indiana still numbered "four to five thousand souls." Timothy Flint, *A Condensed Geography and History of the Western States; or, the Mississippi Valley*, excerpted in Harlow Lindley, ed., *Indiana as Seen by Early Travelers: A Collection of Reprints from Books of Travel, Letters and Diaries Prior to 1830* (Indianapolis: Indiana Historical Commission, 1916), 455; Richard White, writing perceptively of a somewhat earlier time, has also noted the ability of the Indians to shape their destiny by forcing compromises upon the plans of white governments. See Richard White, *The Middle Ground: Indians, Empires, and Republics in the Great Lakes Region, 1650–1815* (Cambridge: Cambridge University Press, 1991), particularly the epilogue, 518–24.

3. John Dillon, *The National Decline of the Miami Indians*, Indiana Historical Society Publications, vol. 1, no. 4 (Indianapolis: Indiana Historical Society, 1897), 141.

4. Stewart Rafert believes Miami numbers were falling steadily since the great epidemic surge of the sixteenth century. Stewart Rafert, *The Miami Indians of Indiana: A Persistent People, 1654–1994* (Indianapolis: Indiana Historical Society, 1996), 3–4. Alan Axelrod believes the same, though he may somewhat overstate the case: "The Miamis, for example, a numerous and proud people in the eighteenth century, had become a diseased, drunken group of 1,000 by 1810." Alan Axelrod, *Chronicle of the Indian Wars from Colonial Times to Wounded Knee* (New York: Prentice Hall, 1993), 130.

5. Contemporary population figures may be found in John Dillon, *A History of Indiana from Its Earliest Exploration by Europeans to the Close of the Territorial Government in 1816* (Indianapolis: Bingham and Doughty, 1859), 579.

6. The treaty also settled unspecified "claims" with a single lump-sum payment to the Delaware of $13,000. See J. Kappler, ed., *Indian Affairs: Laws and Treaties*, vol. 2 (Washington, D.C.: Government Printing Office, 1904), 171. The text of the entire treaty with the Delaware appears on pages 170–71, and the text of the separate agreement with the Miami appears on pages 171–74.

7. J. J. Netterville, ed., *Centennial History of Madison County Indiana: An Account of One Hundred Years of Progress, 1823–1923*, 2 vols. (Anderson, IN: Historians' Association Publishers, 1925), 1:82.

8. There is considerable literature debating the merits and deficiencies of the term as used from the time of Frederick Jackson Turner onward. It is worth noting that it is genuinely contemporary, not an anachronistic imposition, and was used by French, British, and Spanish to describe zones shared by whites and Indians. The author has followed what seem to be the reasonable definitions of the term offered in the discussions in Douglas R. Hurt, *The Indian Frontier* (Albuquerque: University of New Mexico Press, 2002), xii–xiv, and Robert M. Utley, *The Indian Frontier of the American West, 1846–1890* (Albuquerque: University of New Mexico Press, 1984), xviii–xxi.

9. See the account in T. B. Helm, ed., *History of Madison County, Indiana, with Illustrations and Biographical Sketches of Some of Its Prominent Men and Pioneers* (Chicago: Kingman Brothers, 1880), 32. Johnston also thought that as many as 1,000 Delaware remained even after removal, living in scattered bands in Ohio, and that many particularly were settled along the Sandusky River. See Roger James Ferguson, "The White River Indiana Delawares: An Ethnohistoric Synthesis" (PhD diss., Ball State University, 1972), 109, 127.

10. For an account of the inhabitants of the Big Reserve, see Raymond Davis, *Etcetera* (Evansville, IN: Unigraphic, 1971), 29.

11. Bridgie Brill Brelsford, *Indians of Montgomery County, Indiana* (Crawfordsville, IN: Montgomery County Historical Society, 1985), 144–45; Edward H. Chadwick, *History of Shelby County* (Indianapolis: Bowen, 1909), 48; William R. Wepler, "Delaware Subsistence in East Central Indiana," in *Native American Cultures in Indiana: Proceedings of the First Minnetrista Council for Great Lakes Native American Studies*, Ronald Hicks, ed. (Muncie, IN: Minnetrista Cultural Center, 1992), 73.

12. See the discussion of the Census Bureau's standard and the frontier as a zone of "transition" in Robert Mazrim, *The Sangamo Frontier: History and Archaeology in the Shadow of Lincoln* (Chicago: University of Chicago Press, 2007), 18–20. Since Madison County was not yet incorporated, there are no census records pertaining to the county for 1820.

13. Both Netterville, ed., *Centennial History of Madison County Indiana*, 1:70, and Helm, *History of Madison County*, 41, record that the community was not aware of the presence of Logan's band until February 1824.

14. Samuel Woodworth, *Life and Confession of James Hudson, Who Was Executed on Wednesday the 12th January, 1825, at the Falls of Fall Creek for the Murder of Logan, an Indian Chief of the Wyandott Nation* (Indianapolis: Printed at the Gazette Office for the author, 1825), 4–6.

15. O. H. Smith, *Early Indiana Trials and Sketches* (Cincinnati: Moore, Wilstatch and Company, 1858), 51.

16. See John L. Forkner, *A History of Madison County Indiana: A Narrative of Its Historical Progress, Its People, and Its Principal Interests* (Chicago: Lewis Publishing, 1914), 312; Helm, *History of Madison County*, 41; and Netterville, ed., *Centennial History of Madison County Indiana*, 1:70.

17. Leonard U. Hill, ed., *John Johnston and the Indians in the Land of the Three Miamis* (Piqua, 1957), 163.

18. Trial transcript, *State of Indiana v. John Bridge and James Hudson*, Fifth Judicial Circuit, October Session 1824, enclosed in Appeal of Attorneys Martin M. Ray and Calvin Fletcher to Indiana Supreme Court, November Term, 1824, p. 5 (Archives Division, Indiana Commission on Public Records, Indianapolis); Indiana State Supreme Court, November Term, 12th day, 1824, response to the Madison Circuit Court, p. 1, ibid.; Sarah Fletcher to Calvin Fletcher, April 3, 1824, box 1, folder 3, Papers of Calvin Fletcher, M 0108, William Henry Smith Memorial Library, Indiana Historical Society, Indianapolis.

19. Shawnee and Miami in Helm, *History of Madison County*, Netterville, ed., *Centennial History of Madison County Indiana*, and Rafert, *Miami Indians of Indiana*; Miami and Seneca in George Chalou, "Massacre on Fall Creek," *Prologue: The Journal of the National Archives* 4 (Summer 1972) and William M. Osborn, *The Wild Frontier: Atrocities during the American-Indian War from Jamestown Colony to Wounded Knee* (New York: Random House, 2000); Delaware in *Anderson Democrat*, May 1, 1874; Seneca in Brian M. Doerr, "The Massacre at Deer Lick Creek, Madison County, Indiana, 1824," *Indiana Magazine of History* 93 (March 1997), Forkner, *History of Madison County Indiana*, and Hill, ed., *John Johnston and the Indians in the Land of the Three Miamis*.

20. John Johnston to John C. Calhoun, April 28, 1824, Piqua Agency, Letters Received, 1824–1880, Records of the Bureau of Indian Affairs, RG 75, M234, Roll 669, National Archives Microfilm Publications. See also, Hill, ed., *John Johnston and the Indians in the Land of the Three Miamis*, 163.

21. *Pendleton Daily Register*, July 7, 1876.

22. See the discussion in James H. Madison, *The Indiana Way: A State History* (Bloomington: Indiana University Press; Indianapolis: Indiana Historical Society, 1986), 11–12.

23. R. David Edmunds, "Justice on a Changing Frontier: Deer Lick Creek, 1824–1825," *Indiana Magazine of History* 93 (March 1997): 50–51.

24. Charles Johnston, taken on the Ohio River in 1790 for five weeks, was the prisoner of a war band of Shawnee, Mingo (or Iroquois), and Cherokee, who displayed an inclination to intermarriage with one another and even, occasionally, with white captives. See "A Narrative of the Incidents Attending the Capture, Detention and Ransom of Charles Johnston," in *Held Captive by Indians: Selected Narratives, 1642–1836*, Richard VanDerBeets, ed. (Knoxville: University of Tennessee Press, 1973), 272.

25. Rafert, *Miami Indians of Indiana*, 38–39. See also Clinton Alfred Weslager, *The Delaware Indian Westward Migration* (Wallingford, PA: Middle Atlantic Press, 1978).

26. Rafert, *Miami Indians of Indiana*, 35.

27. See the testimony to this in Jacob Piatt Dunn, "The Moravian Mission near Anderson," *Indiana Magazine of History*, 9 (June 1913): 75.

28. White notes the high status and frequent role as mediators between cultures that accrued to Indians of mixed racial background. See White, *Middle Ground*, 213–14. The same phenomenon is noted in R. David Edmunds, *The Potawatomis: Keepers of the Fire* (Norman: University of Oklahoma Press, 1978), 228–29.

29. Rafert, *Miami Indians of Indiana*, 7–12.

30. Lawrence Henry Gipson, *The Moravian Indian Mission on White River* (Indianapolis: Indiana Historical Bureau, 1938), 491.

31. According to local legend, Quakers hid the abolitionist Frederick Douglass in the "Prairie Swamp" after an angry mob chased him out of Pendleton in 1843. See the lengthy notes to the map in *Welcome to Pendleton* (Marion, IN: Walnut Creek Publishing, 2005).

32. A map of this trace and other trails that crossed pioneer Indiana may be found in Brelsford, *Indians of Montgomery County*, 82–83.

33. See the description in Rafert, *Miami Indians of Indiana*, 14.

34. Oliver M. Spencer, *Indian Captivity: A True Narrative of the Capture of the Rev. O. M. Spencer by the Indians, in the Neighbourhood of Cincinnati* (1835; reprint, Ann Arbor: University Microfilms, 1966), 77–78. The captivity narrative became an enormous genre. By 1912 more than three hundred such works had been published in the United States. See David T. Courtwright, *Violent Land: Single Men and Social Disorder from the Frontier to the Inner City* (Cambridge, MA: Harvard University Press, 1996), 114.

35. Sandford C. Cox, *Recollections of the Early Settlement of the Wabash Valley* (Lafayette, IN: Courier Steam, 1860), 18.

36. James Bradley Finley, *Life among the Indians; or, Personal Reminiscences and Historical Incidents Illustrative of Indian Life and Character* (Cincinnati: Curts and Jennings, [1857]), 296–97. Though he is unclear exactly which March month he spent with the Indians, it was within two years of his arrival at his mission in 1821.

37. See the accounts from the Moravian missions cited in Wepler, "Delaware Subsistence in East Central Indiana," 78.

38. Maurice Thompson, *Stories of Indiana* (New York: American Book Company, 1898), 25.

39. Ibid.

40. Finley, *Life among the Indians*, 296.

41. Ibid., 297.

42. George S. Cottman, "Wild Animals of Indiana," *Indiana Magazine of History* 2 (March 1906): 14, and, on the trade in general, R. Carlyle Buley, *The Old Northwest: The Pioneer Period, 1815–1840*, 2 vols. (Indianapolis: Indiana Historical Society, 1950), 1:395–98.

43. This is the ratio given, for example, in Susan Carol Hauser, *Sugartime: The Hidden Pleasures of Making Maple Syrup with a Primer for the Novice Sugarer* (New York: Lyons Press, 1997), 44.

44. Spencer, *Indian Captivity*, 115–16.

45. See the dates for sugar boiling in the years 1802 through 1806 supplied in Table 2, Wepler, "Delaware Subsistence in East Central Indiana," 79.

46. "For weapons, tools, and any number of basic commodities of everyday life, the fur trade had become absolutely crucial." See Daniel K. Richter, *Facing East from Indian Country: A Native History of Early America* (Cambridge, MA: Harvard University Press, 2001), 50.

47. Cass cited in W. L. G. Smith, *Fifty Years of Public Life: The Life and Times of Lewis Cass* (New York: Derby and Jackson, 1856), 170.

48 Paul Chrisler Phillips, "The Fur Trade in the Maumee-Wabash Country," in *Studies in American History Dedicated to James Albert Woodburn* (Bloomington: Indiana University Studies, 1926), 109. This article also reproduces useful inventories of pelts taken in trade.

49. Bruce G. Trigger and William R. Swagerty, "Entertaining Strangers: North America in the Sixteenth Century," in *The Cambridge History of the Native People of the Americas,* vol. 1, *North America*, pt. 1, Bruce G. Trigger and Wilcomb E. Washburn, eds. (Cambridge: Cambridge University Press, 1996), 375–80. On the Civilization Act of 1819, see Michael D. Green, "The Expansion of European Colonization to the Mississippi Valley, 1780–1880," in ibid., 504.

50. Logan Esarey, ed., *Messages and Letters of William Henry Harrison*, 2 vols. (Indianapolis: Indiana Historical Commission, 1922), 71.

51. See Riker and Robertson, eds., *John Tipton Papers*, 1: 12–13

52. A longer list may be found in Ibid., 1: 667–73.

53. Jake Page, writing of the influence of drink on the Indians of New England, states that "Soon enough, here as everywhere on the continent, alcohol addiction became destructive of Indian life—perhaps more destructive than any other European influence besides epidemic disease." Page, *In the Hands of the Great Spirit: The 20,000-Year History of American Indians* (New York: Simon and Schuster, 2003), 175–76.

54. Kluge cited in Andrew R. L. Cayton, *Frontier Indiana* (Bloomington: Indiana University Press, 1996), 198.

55. Johnston cited in "Narrative of the Incidents Attending the Capture, Detention and Ransom of Charles Johnston," 262 and 286.

56. Note the similarity to the behavior of German "order police" battalions in Russia during World War II. They also resorted to heavy drinking to prepare for the slaughter of civilians. Christopher Browning, *Ordinary Men: Reserve Police Battalion 101 and the Final Solution in Poland* (New York: Harper Collins, 1992).

57. McCoy, cited in John D. Barnhart and Donald F. Carmony, *Indiana: From Frontier to Industrial Commonwealth*, 4 vols. (New York: Lewis Historical Publishing Company, 1954), 1:203.

58. This fact was well recognized by many among the Indians themselves. William Anderson, chief of the Delaware at the time of their removal, was in favor of resettling the Delaware to the West so that they would be able to revitalize their traditional ways of living without interference from the whites.

Chapter 3

1. James Whitcomb Riley, "A Child's Home—Long Ago" (1878), in *Little Orphant Annie and Other Poems* (Mineola, NY: Dover, 1994), 11–12

2. James H. Madison, *The Indiana Way: A State History* (Bloomington: Indiana University Press; Indianapolis: Indiana Historical Society, 1986), 73.

3. Some sources place his residence prior to his arrival in Madison County in Kentucky, or Hamilton County, on the Kentucky-Ohio border. Helen Thurman, a descendant of the Bridges

and Harper, places him in Butler County. See Thurman, "The Fall Creek Tragedy," *Indiana Magazine of History* 27 (September 1931). R. David Edmunds, "Justice on a Changing Frontier," *Indiana Magazine of History* 93 (March 1997): 50, places him in Hamilton County, home of the Bridge family, and the anonymous article in the *Anderson Democrat*, May 1, 1874 places him in Kentucky. The Ohio census returns compiled in 1807, following the state's admission in 1803, show a Thomas Harper resident in Butler County, inhabiting a household with two other adult white males. Willard Heiss and R. Thomas Mayhill, eds., *Census of 1807, Butler County, Ohio* (Knightstown, IN: Eastern Publishing Company, 1968), 10.

4. On the volatility and the threat to social order posed by this demographic segment, see the chapter entitled "The Ecology of Frontier Violence," in David T. Courtwright, *Violent Land: Single Men and Social Disorder from the Frontier to the Inner City* (Cambridge, MA: Harvard University Press, 1996), 109–30. For descriptions of Harper, see Brian M. Doerr, "The Massacre at Deer Lick Creek, Madison County, Indiana, 1824," *Indiana Magazine of History* 93 (March 1997): 23, and Thurman, "Fall Creek Tragedy," 231–32.

5. J. J. Netterville, ed., *Centennial History of Madison County Indiana: An Account of One Hundred Years of Progress, 1823–1923*, 2 vols. (Anderson, IN: Historians' Association Publishers, 1925), 1:70.

6. For a detailed account of this atrocity, see Arville L. Funk, *A Sketchbook of Indiana History* (Rochester, IN: Christian Book Press, 1969), 19–22.

7. See Brian W. Dippie, *The Vanishing American* (Lawrence: University Press of Kansas, 1991), 6–8, for the impact of this war on white thinking about the Indians. A hardening of racial hostilities in the region during the 1790s is also remarked in Peter Silver, *Our Savage Neighbors: How Indian War Transformed Early America* (New York: Norton, 2007).

8. *History and Biographical Cyclopaedia of Butler County, Ohio, with Illustrations and Sketches of Its Representative Men and Pioneers* (Cincinnati: Western Biographical Publishing Company, 1882), 414. The census returns collected for the year 1807 in Ohio show three Harpers over the age of twenty-one—John, William, and Thomas—resident in Butler County at that time. See *Census of White Male Inhabitants of over Age 21, Butler County, Ohio, 1807*, in the collection of the Ohio Historical Society, Columbus.

9. The entire story is related in Bert S. Bartlow et al., eds., *Centennial History of Butler County, Ohio: A Comprehensive Compendium of Local Biography and Memoirs of Representative Men and Women of the County* (n.p.: B. F. Bowen and Company, 1905), 348. "About 1798 William Harper settled with his family on section 19 (Wayne Township). In the spring of the year 1800, in sugar-making time, the Indians came in quite a number to visit the Harpers, as they were accustomed to do. An old squaw became very intimate with the family, especially with little Elizabeth, a three-year-old child. One evening Mrs. Harper sent two children to bring in the cows, and their three-year-old sister followed. When they had gone some distance the little girl cried for them to stop, but in their hurry they gave her no attention. After returning home Elizabeth was missing. Search was immediately instituted, but the little girl could not be found. The next morning little footprints were found in the mud where she had crossed a stream, and close by them moccasin tracks. The Indians were all gone, and it was evident the babe had been stolen. The father and mother visited all the Indian camps in search of their child, who was never found. In 1842 a gentleman who was well acquainted with the Harpers saw Elizabeth. He knew her by the family likeness, which they all possessed to a remarkable degree. She had married an Indian warrior and had two children. She afterward went with her tribe west of the Mississippi and was never heard of again. Her parents had died years before, after despairing of ever finding her."

10. Although most sources credit Bridge with nine children by his deceased Harper wife, the census of 1820, in which the territory of the New Purchase is listed as "Delaware County," shows the household with eight dependent children—five boys and three girls—in addition to the head of the household. See Willard Heiss, ed., *1820 Federal Census for Indiana* (Indianapolis: Indiana Historical Society, 1966), 45.

11. On both men, see Sandford C. Cox, *Recollections of the Early Settlement of the Wabash Valley* (Lafayette, IN: Courier Steam, 1860), 9; Doerr, "Massacre at Deer Lick Creek," 22; and Thurman, "Fall Creek Tragedy," 232–33.

12. See Mary M. Crawford, "Mrs. Lydia B. Bacon's Journal, 1811–1812," *Indiana Magazine of History* 40 (December 1944): 367–86.

13. James Hall, cited in Barnhart and Carmony, *Indiana*, 1:220.

14. On the sale of public lands in the Indiana Territory see ibid., 223–25; Madison, *Indiana Way*, 122–26; and Paul W. Gates, "Land Policy and Tenancy in the Prairie Counties of Indiana," *Indiana Magazine of History* 35 (1939): 1–26.

15. John Dillon, *A History of Indiana from Its Earliest Exploration by Europeans to the Close of the Territorial Government in 1816* (Indianapolis: Bingham and Doughty, 1859), 564.

16. Madison, *Indiana Way*, 63.

17. Immogene B. Brown, comp., *Land Records of Indiana (Recorded in the District Land Offices) Madison County* (Anderson: Privately printed, 1965), 96. For details on the surveying of the lands of the Northwest Territory, and its conversion thereby into an easily transferable commodity, see Andro Linklater, *Measuring America: How an Untamed Wilderness Shaped the United States and Fulfilled the Promise of Democracy* (New York: Walker and Company, 2002), especially 160–75.

18. For an informative account of the timber of the forests of Indiana and its varied uses, see Logan Esarey, *Indiana Home* (Bloomington: Indiana University Press, 1976), 26–40.

19. Nathan Smith to Joshua Atwood, April 27, 1824, Nathan Smith Letter, SC 1370, William Henry Smith Memorial Library, Indiana Historical Society, Indianapolis.

20. See Louis B. Ewbank, "Building a Pioneer Home," *Indiana Magazine of History* 40 (June 1944): 111–28; and James Albert Woodburn, "Local Life and Color in the New Purchase," ibid. 9 (September 1913): 222–23.

21. William C. Latta, *Outline History of Indiana Agriculture* (Lafayette, IN: Purdue University Press, 1938), 42–120.

22. John Modell, "Family and Fertility on the Indiana Frontier, 1820," *American Quarterly* 23 (1971): 615–34.

23. William Warren Sweet, *Circuit-Rider Days in Indiana* (Indianapolis: W. K. Stewart Company, 1916), 79–80. See also John C. Smith, *Reminiscences of Early Methodism in Indiana* (Indianapolis: J. M. Olcott, 1879), 38–40.

24. Madison, *Indiana Way*, 103.

25. Note, for instance, the letters of Sarah Fletcher to her husband Calvin during his days in Madison County. Nearly every communication opens with discussions of the varied fevers and illnesses of their children. See box 1, folder 3, Calvin Fletcher Papers, M 0108, William Henry Smith Memorial Library.

26. See the estimates in Barnhart and Carmony, *Indiana*, 1:251, and W. D. Gatch, "The Health of Our Pioneer Ancestors," in *Indiana Pioneer Stories*, vol. 1, Doris Leistner, ed. (New Albany, IN: D. Leistner, 2002), 320.

27. John Bartlow Martin, *Indiana: An Interpretation* (New York: Knopf, 1947), 31–32.

28. Philip D. Jordan, "The Death of Nancy Hanks Lincoln," *Indiana Magazine of History* 40 (June 1944): 103–10.

29. Gayle Thornbrough, Dorothy Riker, and Paula Corpuz, eds., *The Diary of Calvin Fletcher*, 9 vols. (Indianapolis: Indiana Historical Society, 1972–83), 1:94–95.

30. See the discussion and table in Courtwright, *Violent Land*, 81–84. See also the discussion of Western violence in Richard White, *"It's Your Misfortune and None of My Own": A History of the American West* (Norman: University of Oklahoma Press, 1991), 337–40.

31. *Anderson Democrat*, May 1, 1874.

32. J. A. Wertz, *The Town of Pendleton, Together with a Sketch of Its Early History* (Anderson, IN: Brandon-Benham, 1896), 3–4.

33. William C. Smith, *Indiana Miscellany: Consisting of Sketches of Indian Life, the Early Settlement, Customs, and Hardships of the People, and the Introduction of the Gospel and Schools, Together with Biographical Notices of the Pioneer Methodist Preachers of the State* (Cincinnati: Poe and Hitchcock, 1867), 27–28; Samuel Woodworth, *The Life and Confession of James Hudson, Who Was Executed on Wednesday the 12th January, 1825, at the Falls of Fall Creek for the Murder of Logan, an Indian Chief of the Wyandott Nation* (Indianapolis: Printed at the Gazette Office for the author, 1825), 3.

34. Woodworth, *Life and Confession of James Hudson*, 4–5.

35. Ibid., 6.

36. Ibid., 7.

37. Ibid., 10.

38. Thurman, "Fall Creek Tragedy," 230.

39. Ibid., 234.

40. Woodworth, *Life and Confession of James Hudson*, 6.

41. Ibid.

42. Ibid., 7.

43. Ibid., 8.

Chapter 4

1. Xenophon, *The Persian Expedition* (New York: Penguin, 1949), 145.

2. Some accounts name the youth as "Jesse" Adams, but that of his own granddaughter refers to his name as "John." Compare the accounts in *Pendleton Daily Register*, July 7, 1876, with that by Adams's grandchild in the *Anderson Democrat*, May 1, 1874.

3. Hudson reports the presence of young Adams at the Bridge cabin on the night of the killings, and S. N. Sargent reports the observations made by the boy (Sargent's grandfather).

4. *Pendleton Daily Register*, July 7, 1876.

5. Samuel Woodworth, *The Life and Confession of James Hudson, Who Was Executed on Wednesday the 12th January, 1825, at the Falls of Fall Creek for the Murder of Logan, an Indian Chief of the Wyandott Nation* (Indianapolis: Printed at the Gazette Office for the author, 1825), 15.

6. *Anderson Democrat*, May 1, 1874.

7. Woodworth, *Confession of James Hudson*, 15–16.

8. *Anderson Democrat*, May 1, 1874.

9. Woodworth, *Life and Confession of James Hudson*, 16. According to one local account at the time, the property of the Indians was still at the camp at the time of the visit by Adams and the killers, but it disappeared between then and the arrival of Tharp's investigative party. This appears in the *Washington (NY) Republican and Congressional Examiner*, April 19, 1824, but it seems unlikely to be true. Hudson himself reported that Harper and the others left the Indian

camp the day of the murders carrying Indian belongings, and the bodies of the dead, by several accounts, were found stripped naked. The surname of Sheriff Samuel Cory is rendered variously in the sources as "Corey" and "Corry."

10. *Washington (NY) Republican and Congressional Examiner*, April 19, 1824.

11. See, for example, similarly lurid accounts such as that recorded at the time of the killing of six white women and children by the Indian "Samuel Mohawk" in 1843. Using only a stone and a club for his weapons, Mohawk brutalized his victims, later volunteering to show authorities "the mangled bodies of his victims." The contemporary account is recorded in John F. Gall and David K. Webb, *The Massacre of the Wigton Family, with an Account of the Trial of Samuel Mohawk, the Murderer* (Chillicothe, OH: Privately printed, 1934), 5, in the collection of the Ohio Historical Society, Columbus.

12. *Pendleton Daily Register*, July 7, 1876.

13. Woodworth, *Life and Confession of James Hudson*, 16.

14. Sanford C. Cox, *Recollections of the Early Settlement of the Wabash Valley* (Lafayette, IN: Courier Steam, 1860), 10; John Forkner and Byron Dyson, *Historical Sketches and Reminiscences of Madison County, Indiana* ([Logansport, IN: Press of Wilson Humphreys and Company], 1897), 27–28; J. A. Wertz, *The Town of Pendleton, Together with a Sketch of Its Early History* (Anderson, IN: Brandon-Benahm, 1896), 5; Woodworth, *Life and Confession of James Hudson*, 17–18. For the improbable local tradition on the celerity of his flight, see B. R. Sulgrove, ed., *History of Indianapolis and Marion County, Indiana* (Philadelphia: L. H. Everts and Company, 1884), 55.

15. In his recollections John Johnston passes the judgment on Texas. See Leonard U. Hill, ed., *John Johnston and the Indians in the Land of the Three Miamis* (Piqua, 1957), 162. Ohio is given as Harper's destination in Woodworth, *Life and Confession of James Hudson*, contemporary news accounts, O. H. Smith, *Early Indiana Trials and Sketches* (Cincinnati: Moore, Wilstatch, Keys and Company, 1858), 52, and many other sources. Kentucky is given in the local reminiscences recounted in the *Anderson Democrat*, May 1, 1874.

16. *A History and Biographical Cyclopaedia of Butler County, Ohio, with Illustrations and Sketches of Its Representative Men and Pioneers* (Cincinnati: Western Biographical Publishing, 1882), 415.

17. Cox, *Recollections of the Early Settlement of the Wabash Valley*, 10.

18. By 1820, according to an early source, "A sense of security pervaded the minds of the people. The hostile Indian tribes, having been overpowered, humbled, and impoverished, no longer excited the fears of the pioneer settlers, who dwelt in safety in their plain log cabin homes, and cultivated their small fields without the protection of armed sentinels." John Dillon, *A History of Indiana from Its Earliest Exploration by Europeans to the Close of the Territorial Government in 1816* (Indianapolis: Bingham and Doughty, 1859), 563.

19. The *Richmond Public Leger* and *Indianapolis Gazette* both had stories on the killings within a few days. Within the month, an account from the *Gazette* appeared as far east as the *Washington (NY) Republican and Congressional Examiner*, and, as Brian Doerr notes, in the *Hillsborough (NC) Recorder* (Doerr, "The Massacre at Deer Lick Creek, Madison County, Indiana, 1824," *Indiana Magazine of History* 93 [March 1997]: 29).

20. *Terre Haute Western Register*, April 7, 1824; *Pendleton Daily Register*, July 7, 1876; *Indianapolis Gazette*, March 30, 1824; Doerr, "Massacre at Deer Lick Creek," 29.

21. For a good overview of the origins and significance of the "brief orgy of irresponsibility, cruelty and despair that was Lord Dunmore's War," see Anthony F. C. Wallace, *The Death and Rebirth of the Seneca* (1969; reprint, New York: Random House, 1972), 123–25.

22. As John Johnston described them to an interviewer some decades later, "the Dela-

wares—very implacable, the most so of any of the North Western Indians." See "Death of Col. Wm. Crawford as Told to Lyman C. Draper," June 1843, p. 20, Draper MSS, vol. 11YY, Piqua Historical Site, Piqua, OH.

23. Hill, ed., *John Johnston and the Indians in the Land of the Three Miamis*, 163.

24. Ibid., 11–13; Francis Paul Prucha, *The Great Father: The United States Government and the American Indians* (Lincoln: University of Nebraska Press, 1984), 35–40.

25. On the role of the agents in general, see Prucha, *Great Father*, 56–60. For the controversy surrounding William Wells, and the friction between Wells and Johnston, see Hill, ed., *John Johnston and the Indians in the Land of the Three Miamis*, 28–29.

26. Charlotte Reeve Conover, *Concerning the Forefathers: Being a Memoir, with Personal Narrative and Letters of Two Pioneers Col. Robert Patterson and Col. John Johnston the Paternal and Maternal Grandfathers of John Henry Patterson of Dayton, Ohio, for Whose Children This Book Is Written* (Dayton, OH: National Cash Register Company, 1902), 41.

27. Logan Esarey, *History of Indiana from Its Exploration to 1922* (Dayton, OH: Dayton Historical Publishing, 1924), 368.

28. Conover, *Concerning the Forefathers*, 27. From the time of John Quincy Adams's, candidacy, at the least, Johnston regarded Andrew Jackson's vision of political culture as incompatible with true democracy. See his comment on the election of 1824 in Andrew R. L. Cayton, *The Frontier Republic: Ideology and Politics in the Ohio Country, 1780–1825* (Kent, OH: Kent State University Press, 1986), 136.

29. See John Johnston to Dr. Daniel Drake, December 3, 1811, p. 25, Draper MSS, vol. 11YY, Piqua Historical Site. "I have at length procured you the Head of an Indian not many years dead, as there is no opportunity upon this place at present to forward it."

30. Ibid., 51, and Wallace, *Death and Rebirth of the Seneca*, 123. As will be seen at the sentencing of the convicted killers, it was widely believed that the Logan killed at Fall Creek was a blood relation of Chief Logan, "the Great Mingo," who famously avenged his people in Lord Dunmore's War. Many, however, dispute this. See John A. Rayner, ed., *The First Century of Piqua Ohio* (Piqua, OH: Magee Brothers, 1916), 249. "This is the third Indian 'Logan' in our history of the north-west territory, all of whom were of different tribes, and not in any way related."

31. Hill, ed., *John Johnston and the Indians in the Land of the Three Miamis*, 110.

32. Seneca chiefs to Secretary of War Calhoun, February 19, 1824, Records of the Bureau of Indian Affairs, Piqua Agency, Letters Received, RG 75, M234, roll 669, National Archives Microfilm Publication (hereafter cited as "Piqua agency"). Parts of this letter are also reprinted in *The Papers of John C. Calhoun*, 28 vols. (Columbia: University of South Carolina Press, 1959–2003), 8:548–49.

33. Roger James Ferguson, "The White River Indiana Delawares: An Ethnohistoric Synthesis" (PhD diss., Ball State University, 1972), 109–10.

34. Charles Dickens, *American Notes*, in *The Works of Charles Dickens*, vol. 5 (New York: Colliers, n.d.), 323–24.

35. *Papers of John C. Calhoun*, 9: 62–63

36. For example, see Johnston's account of the torture, execution, posthumous mutilation, and consumption of Colonel William Crawford at the hands of an aggrieved band of Delaware warriors. Col. John Johnston to Lyman C. Draper, June 1843, p. 20, Draper MSS, vol. 11YY, Piqua Historical Site.

37. John Johnston to William Lee, 2nd Auditor of the U.S. Treasury, Piqua, September 14, 1824, John Johnston Correspondence, 1815–1842, VFM 3505, Ohio Historical Society

Archives, Columbus. Noting a letter he received in July from Lee, he comments, "Bad health has prevented me from replying to it sooner." John Johnston to John C. Calhoun, May 19, 1824, "Piqua agency." In the same letter, he also notes the unusually heavy precipitation in this spring. It should be noted as well that Johnston was regarded by some of his contemporaries as a noted hypochondriac: Andy Hite (historic site manager), interview with the author, August 9, 2007, Piqua Historical Site. Many of the complaints about Johnston's misuse of public funds may be found in volume 9 of the *Papers of John C. Calhoun*. Such allegations were common against the Indian agents. John Tipton, agent at Fort Wayne, Gad Humphreys, an agent in New York State, and many others all faced allegations, generally unproved, at various times. See, for example, the letters on Humphreys's use of government funds in *Papers of John C. Calhoun*, 8:501–2.

38. Forkner and Dyson, *Historical Sketches and Reminiscences of Madison County*, 28.

39. Johnston to Calhoun, May 19, 1824.

40. See, for example, the accounts of the attacks on Indians in 1809 and 1810, prior to statehood, in which Indian delegations accepted compensation in kind for grievous injury, which are recounted in William C. Smith, *Indiana Miscellany: Consisting of Sketches of Indian Life, the Early Settlement, Customs and Hardships of the People, and the Introduction of the Gospel and of Schools, Together with Biographical Notices of the Pioneer Methodist Preachers in the State* (Cincinnati: Poe and Hitchcock, 1867), 28–30.

41. Thomas McKenny to John Johnston, May 11, 1824, cited in Herman Viola, *Thomas L. McKenney: Architect of America's Indian Policy, 1816–1830* (Chicago: Sage Books, 1974), 183, and George Chalou, "Massacre on Fall Creek," *Prologue: The Journal of the National Archives* 4 (Summer 1972): 110. On the founding of the Bureau of Indian Affairs, which was confirmed in 1832 by Congress, see Prucha, *Great Father*, 59–60.

42. See the list of travel times in Timothy Crumrin, ed., *A Hoosier Miscellany: A Collection of Tales, Trivia and Tidbits about Early Indiana* (Fishers, IN: Conner Prairie, 1997), 9.

43. On Conner's life and career, see John Lauritz Larson and David G. Vanderstel, "Agent of Empire: William Conner on the Indiana Frontier, 1800–1855," *Indiana Magazine of History* 80 (December 1984): 301–28; Charles N. Thompson, *Sons of the Wilderness: John and William Conner* (Indianapolis: Indiana Historical Society, 1937); and Clinton Alfred Weslager, *The Delaware Indian Westward Migration* (Wallingford, PA: Middle Atlantic Press, 1978), 361–62. His marriage with Mekinges is also the subject of a short opera and accompanying book. Denise Page Caraher, *The End of Forever* (Zionsville, IN: Guild Press/Emmis Books, 2003). Local pride in Conner was strong and led to some historical misunderstanding. A history of Hamilton County (site of the Conner estate) from the nineteenth century, for example, declares, "He had long resided with the Shawanoes, and was also very familiar with the manners, customs and usages of both tribes, and with the White Water, White River and Wabash tribes generally. His word was law with all of them. In the case of the killing of Indians in the spring of 1824, for which Hudson and others perished on the gallows, it was chiefly through his instrumentality and interposition that the laws of the State were permitted to be executed in due course without the interference of the adjacent Indians, whose custom it was to take such matters into their own hands and mete out savage retribution upon the perpetrators of the outrage upon their race." As concerns the aftermath of Fall Creek, this is an unsupportable and inflated assessment of Conner's role. See T. B. Helm, ed., *History of Hamilton County, Indiana, with Illustrations and Biographical Sketches of Some of Its Prominent Men and Pioneers* (Chicago: Kingman Brothers, 1880), 34.

44. Lewis Cass to John Johnston, May 3, 1824, M234, roll 419, Michigan Superintendency (emphases in original).

45. Johnston to Calhoun, May 19, 1824; Johnston to Cass, May 13, 1824, M1, roll 14, Michigan Superintendency.

46. Johnston to Calhoun, May 19, 1824.

Chapter 5

1. John Johnston to Thomas McKenney, October 19, 1824, John Johnston, selected Documents and letters, 1805–1843, roll 1, no. 33, Ohio Historical Society, Columbus.

2. John Johnston to Lewis Cass, May 29, 1824, M1, roll 14, Michigan Superintendency.

3. Johnston to Cass, May 13, 1824, ibid.

4. Hendricks cited in Frederick Dinsmore Hill, "William Hendricks: Indiana Politician and Western Advocate, 1812–1850" (PhD diss., Indiana University, 1972), 100.

5. Harrison cited in R. David Edmunds, "Justice on a Changing Frontier: Deer Lick Creek, 1824–1825," *Indiana Magazine of History* 93 (1997): 48.

6. O. H. Smith, *Early Indiana Trials and Sketches* (Cincinnati: Moore, Wilstatch, Keys and Company, 1858), 52.

7. John H. B. Nowland, *Early Reminiscences of Indianapolis, with Short Biographical Sketches of Its Early Citizens, and a Few of the Prominent Business Men of the Present* Day (Indianapolis: Sentinel Book and Job Printing House, 1870), 137.

8. For descriptions of Winchell's character, see Smith, *Early Indiana Trials and Sketches*, 53, and J. J. Netterville, ed., *Centennial History of Madison County Indiana: An Account of One Hundred Years of Progress, 1823–1923*, 2 vols. (Anderson, IN: Historians' Association Publishers, 1925), 1:73.

9. Samuel Harden, *History of Madison County* (Markleville, IN, 1874), 247.

10. Netterville, ed., *Centennial History of Madison County Indiana*, 1:73, and John Forkner and Byron Dyson, *Historical Sketches and Reminiscences of Madison County, Indiana* ([Logansport, IN: Press of Wilson, Humphreys and Company], 1897), 28.

11. Sanford C. Cox, *Recollections of the Early Settlement of the Wabash Valley* (Lafayette, IN: Courier Steam, 1860), 10.

12. John Johnston, "Estimate of Expenses," December 21, 1824, John Johnston, Selected Documents and Letters, 1805–1843, roll 1, no. 33.

13. Hendricks's praise, and his assessment of Johnston's motives for not removing the prisoners, in Hendricks to Johnston, copy, June 1824, ibid.

14. John Johnston to Thomas McKenney, October 19, 1824, ibid.

15. Johnston to McKenney, February 1, 1826, Records of the Bureau of Indian Affairs, Piqua Agency, Letters Received, RG 75, M234, roll 669, National Archives Microfilm Publication (hereafter cited as "Piqua agency").

16. Immogene B. Brown, comp., *Land Records of Indiana (Recorded in the District Land Offices) Madison County* (Anderson, IN: Privately printed, 1965), 2:516.

17. Jacob Piatt Dunn Jr., *Greater Indianapolis: The History, the Industries, the Institutions, and the People of a City of Homes*, 2 vols. (Chicago: Lewis Publishing Company, 1910), 1:554, 2:643–45.

18. Francis M. Trissal, *Public Men of Indiana: A Political History*, 2 vols. (Hammond: G. B. Conkey, 1922), 1:13, and B. R. Sulgrove, ed., *History of Indianapolis and Marion County, Indiana* (Philadelphia: L. H. Everts and Company, 1884), 185.

19. Forkner and Dyson, *Historical Sketches and Reminiscences of Madison County*, 28.

20. Much of Johnston's correspondence with John Calhoun on the selection may be found in volume 9 of *The Papers of John C. Calhoun*, 28 vols. (Columbia: University of South Carolina

Press, 1959–2003), especially 9:103 (John Johnston to John Calhoun, May 19, 1824) and 9:346 (John Johnston to McKenney, October 9, 1824).

21. John Bartlow Martin, *Indiana: An Interpretation* (New York: Knopf, 1947), 36.

22. On Noble's life and career, see Nina K. Reid, "James Noble," *Indiana Magazine of History* 9 (March 1913): 1–13.

23. Johnston to McKenney, February 1, 1826, "Piqua agency." As Reid states in her biographical note on Noble, a number of his contemporaries enjoyed greater renown as masters of the law, "but none of them could equal him in making a stump speech or addressing a jury. He had a very strong voice so that people within several squares of the courthouse could tell when he was speaking." Reid, "James Noble," 2.

24. Dunn, *Greater Indianapolis*, 1:508.

25. John H. B. Nowland, *Sketches of Prominent Citizens of 1876, with a Few of the Pioneers of the City Who Have Passed Away* (Indianapolis: Tilford and Carlon, 1877), 157; George Pence, "Philip Sweester and His times," *Indiana Magazine of History* 23 (December 1927): 378–92.

26. Dunn, *Greater Indianapolis*, 1:372.

27. See, for example, James Noble to Calvin Fletcher, March 21, 1824, box 1, folder 3, Calvin Fletcher Papers, M 0108, William Henry Smith Memorial Library, Indiana Historical Society, Indianapolis.

28. Records of their transactions may be found throughout Brown, *Land Records of Indiana*, and in Jane E. Darlington, *Marion County, Indiana: Complete Probate Records 1830–1852* (Indianapolis: Jane E. Darlington, 1994), 306; Donald Carmony, *Indiana, 1816–1830: The Pioneer Era* (Indianapolis: Indiana Historical Bureau and Indiana Historical Society, 1998), 112.

29. Sarah Fletcher to Calvin Fletcher, April 3, 1824, box 1, folder 3, Fletcher Papers. Local blacks, according to early sources, "venerated" Fletcher for his support for the cause of freedom. See William Wesley Woollen, *Biographical and Historical Sketches of Early Indiana* (Indianapolis: Hammond and Company, 1883), 466.

30. Netterville, ed., *Centennial History of Madison County Indiana*, 1:74; Trial transcript, *State of Indiana v. John Bridge and James Hudson*, Fifth Judicial Circuit, October Session 1824, enclosed in appeal of attorneys Martin M. Ray and Calvin Fletcher to Indiana Supreme Court, November Term, 1824 (Archives Division, Indiana Commission on Public Records, Indianapolis).

31. *Pendleton Daily Register*, July 7, 1876.

32. Netterville, ed., *Centennial History of Madison County Indiana*, 1:74; Smith, *Early Indiana Trials and Sketches*, 56.

33. Trial transcript.

34. See the accounts in George Chalou, "Massacre on Fall Creek," *Prologue: The Journal of the National Archives* 4 (Summer 1972): 111, or Smith, *Early Indiana Trials and Sketches*, 56, for examples.

35. Nowland, *Early Reminiscences of Indianapolis*, 92.

36. Smith, *Early Indiana Trials and Sketches*, 56.

37. Ibid., 56–57.

38. Ibid., 57.

39. Johnston to McKenney, October 19, 1824, "Piqua agency."

40. Trial transcript; Johnston to McKenney, October 19, 1824.

41. Jacob Piatt Dunn, *True Indian Stories* (Indianapolis: Sentinel Print Company, 1908), 204.

42. *Bloomington Gazette*, November 13, 1824.

43. Trial transcript.

44. Johnston to McKenney, October 19, 1824.

45. Indiana State Supreme Court, November Term, 12th Day 1824, Order Book 2, 1823–1828, Indiana State Archives.

46. The account of Hudson's escape and recapture is based primarily upon Samuel Woodworth, *Life and Confession of James Hudson, Who Was Executed on Wednesday the 12th January, 1825, at the Falls of Fall Creek for the Murder of Logan, an Indian Chief of the Wyandott Nation* (Indianapolis: Printed at the Gazette Office for the author, 1825), 19–21.

47. Johnston to Noble, December 21, 1824, "Piqua agency."

48. The letter is reprinted in Woodworth, *Life and Confession of James Hudson*, appendix.

49. Ibid., 22.

50. Cox, *Recollections of the Early Settlement of the Wabash Valley*, 10–11.

51. Martin, *Indiana*, 38.

52. Logan Esarey, "Pioneer Politics," *Indiana Magazine of History* 13 (June 1917): 124–25.

53. Carmony, *Indiana*, 444, 550; William C. Smith, *Indiana Miscellany: Consisting of Sketches of Indian Life, the Early Settlement, Customs and Hardships of the People, and the Introduction of the Gospel and of Schools, Together with Biographical Notices of the Pioneer Methodist Preachers of the State* (Cincinnati: Poe and Hitchcock, 1867), 236–38.

54. *Indianapolis Journal*, May 17, 1825.

55. Smith, *Early Indiana Trials and Sketches*, 177.

56. *Brookville Inquirer*, May 25, 1825.

57. Smith, *Early Indiana Trials and Sketches*, 177.

58. Netterville, ed., *Centennial History of Madison County Indiana*, 1:76.

59. Ibid., 1:77–78. George Chalou accepts this interpretation. See Chalou, "Massacre on Fall Creek," 113.

60. *Indianapolis Journal*, May 17, 1825.

61. Ibid.

62. Smith, *Early Indiana Trials and Sketches*, 178.

63. Netterville, ed., *Centennial History of Madison County Indiana*, 1:76.

64. *Indianapolis Journal*, May 17, 1825.

65. Netterville, ed., *Centennial History of Madison County Indiana*, 1:76.

66. Smith, *Early Indiana Trials and Sketches*, 178.

67. *Brookville Inquirer*, May 25, 1825; *Indianapolis Journal*, May 17, 1825; Netterville, ed., *Centennial History of Madison County Indiana*, 1:76–77.

68. Smith, *Early Indiana Trials and Sketches*, 179.

69. Secretary of State, Petitions, 1825–1857, box 9, folder 6, Indiana State Archives. A copy of the text of the petition, without the appended signatures, in Dorothy Riker and Gayle Thornbrough, eds., *Messages and Papers Relating to the Administration of James Brown Ray, Governor of Indiana, 1825–1831* (Indianapolis: Indiana Historical Bureau, 1954), 38–39.

70. Leonard U. Hill, ed., *John Johnston and the Indians in the Land of the Three Miamis* (Piqua, OH, 1957), 163–64.

71. *Indianapolis Gazette*, June 7, 1825.

72. Nowland, *Early Reminiscences of Indianapolis*, 166.

73. Idid.

74. Maurice Thompson, *Stories of Indiana* (New York: American Book Company, 1898), 196.

75. Esarey, "Pioneer Politics," 124; Thompson, *Stories of Indiana*, 196.

76. Thompson, *Stories of Indiana*, 196–97. The pardon is included in Dorothy Riker, ed., *Executive Proceedings of the State of Indiana, 1816–1836* (Indianapolis: Indiana Historical Bureau, 1947), 321.

77. *Indianapolis Gazette*, June 7, 1825.

78. Johnston to McKenney, June 10, 1825, "Piqua agency."

79. *Pendleton Daily Register*, July 7, 1876.

Aftermath

1. Augustine, *The Confessions*, John K. Ryan, trans. (New York: doubleday, 1960, 236–37.

2. Leonard U. Hill, ed., *John Johnston and the Indians in the Land of the Three Miamis* (Piqua, OH, 1957), 164; Charlotte Reeve Conover, *Concerning the Forefathers: Being a Memoir with Personal Narrative and Letters of Two Pioneers Col. Robert Patterson and Col. John Johnston, the Paternal and Maternal Grandfathers of John Henry Patterson of Dayton, Ohio for Whose Children This Book Is Written* (Dayton, OH: National Cash Register Company, 1902), 56.

3. John Bartlow Martin, *Indiana: An Interpretation* (New York: Knopf, 1947), 39.

4. *Indianapolis Journal*, June 7, 1825.

5. Brian M. Doerr, "The Massacre at Deer Lick Creek, Madison County, Indiana, 1824," *Indiana Magazine of History* 93 (March 1997): 45–46.

6. The removal of the last remnants of native tribes from Indiana went on for a generation more. See Phyllis Gernhardt, "'Justice and Public Policy': Indian Trade, Treaties, and Removal from Northern Indiana, 1826–1846," in *The Boundaries between Us: Natives and Newcomers along the Frontiers of the Old Northwest Territory, 1750–1850*, Daniel P. Barr, ed. (Kent, OH: Kent State University Press, 2006), 178–95.

7. The same remained largely true in the case of interracial homicides involving whites and blacks at the time. Although some slave state legal codes provided the same penalty for killing a slave as killing a free man, in practice juries typically convicted whites in such cases of manslaughter rather than murder. See the cases discussed in Boynton Merrill Jr., *Jefferson's Nephews: A Frontier Tragedy* (Lincoln: University of Nebraska Press, 2004). Interestingly, Indians accused of murder also sometimes utilized frontier law to evade capital sentences. See Bruce P. Smith, "Negotiating Law on the Frontier: Responses to Cross-cultural Homicide in Illinois, 1810–1815," in Barr, ed., *Boundaries between Us*, 173.

Selected Bibliography

Manuscripts

Archives Division, Indiana Commission on Public Records, Indianapolis.
    State of Indiana v. John Bridge and James Hudson, Fifth Circuit, October Session 1824, enclosed in appeal of attorneys Martin M. Ray and Calvin Fletcher to Indiana Supreme Court, November Term, 1824.
    Indiana State Supreme Court, November Term, 12th Day, 1824, response to the Madison Circuit Court.
    Secretary of State: Petitions, 1825–1857.
Ohio Historical Society Archives, Columbus.
    John Johnston Correspondence, 1815–1842, VFM 3505.
Piqua Historical Site, Piqua, Ohio.
    Draper MSS, vol. 11YY.
    Papers of John Johnston.
William Henry Smith Memorial Library, Indiana Historical Society, Indianapolis.
    John Johnston Records, 1802–1811, BV 2611.
    Calvin Fletcher Papers, M 0108.
    Nathan Smith Letter, SC 1370.
    James Brown Ray, SC 1890.
United States National Archives, Washington, D.C.
    Records of the Bureau of Indian Affairs, RG 75, National Archives Microfilm Publications M234, Roll 669, Piqua Agency, Letters Received, 1824–1880.

Books, articles, and dissertations

Anonymous. *Welcome to Pendleton*. Marion, IN: Walnut Creek Publishing, 2005.
Axelrod, Alan. *Chronicle of the Indian Wars from Colonial Times to Wounded Knee*. New York: Prentice Hall, 1993.
Barnhart, John D., and Donald F. Carmony. *Indiana: From Frontier to Industrial Commonwealth*. 4 vols. New York: Lewis Historical Publishing Company, 1954.
Barr, Daniel P., ed. *The Boundaries between Us: Natives and Newcomers along the Frontiers of the Old Northwest Territory, 1750–1850*. Kent, OH: Kent State University Press, 2006.
Bartlow, Bert S., et al., eds. *Centennial History of Butler County Ohio*. N. p. : B. F. Bowen and Company, 1905.
Brelsford, Bridgie Brill. *Indians of Montgomery County, Indiana*. Crawfordsville, IN: Montgomery County Historical Society, 1985.
Brown, Immogene B., comp. *Land Records of Indiana (Recorded in the District Land Offices) Madison County*. Anderson, IN: Privately printed, 1965.
———. *Madison County, Indiana: Information Abstracted from Deed Records, 1824 thru 1840*. Anderson, IN, 1980.
Browning, Christopher R. *Ordinary Men: Reserve Police Battalion 101 and the Final Solution in Poland*. New York: Harper Collins, 1992.
Buley, R. Carlyle. *The Old Northwest: Pioneer Period, 1815–1840*. 2 vols. Indianapolis: Indiana Historical Society, 1950.
Calloway, Colin G. *The Shawnees and the War for America*. New York: Viking, 2007.

Caraher, Denise Page. *The End of Forever: The Story of Mekinges and William Conner.* Zionsville, IN: Guild Press/Emmis Books, 2003.

Cayton, Andrew R. L. *Frontier Indiana.* Bloomington: Indiana University Press, 1996.

———. *The Frontier Republic: Ideology and Politics in the Ohio Country, 1780–1825.* Kent, OH: Kent State University Press, 1986.

Chadwick, Edward H. *History of Shelby County, Indiana.* Indianapolis: B. F. Bowen and Company, 1909.

Chalou, George. "Massacre on Fall Creek." *Prologue: The Journal of the National Archives* 4 (Summer 1972): 109–14.

Chapel, Charles Edward. *Guns of the Old West: An Illustrated Guide.* 1962. Reprint, Mineola, NY: Dover Publications, 2002.

Conover, Charlotte Reeve. *Concerning the Forefathers: Being a Memoir, with Personal Narrative and Letters of Two Pioneers Col. Robert Patterson and Col. John Johnston, the Paternal and Maternal Grandfathers of John Henry Patterson of Dayton, Ohio, for Whose Children This Book Is Written.* Dayton, OH: National Cash Register Company, 1902.

Conrad, Joseph. *Under Western Eyes.* New York: Random House, 2001.

Cottman, George S. "Wild Animals of Indiana." *Indiana Magazine of History* 2 (March 1906): 14–20.

Cox, Sandford C. *Recollections of the Early Settlement of the Wabash Valley.* Lafayette, IN: Courier Steam, 1860.

Crumrin, Timothy, ed. *A Hoosier Miscellany: A Collection of Tales, Trivia, and Tidbits about Early Indiana.* Fishers, IN: Conner Prairie, 1997.

Darlington, Jane E. *Marion County, Indiana: Complete Probate Records, 1830–1852.* Indianapolis: Jane E. Darlington, 1994.

Davis, Raymond. *Etcetera.* Evansville, IN: Unigraphic, 1971.

Dickens, Charles. *American Notes.* In *The Works of Charles Dickens*, vol. 5. New York: Colliers, n.d.

Dillon, John. *A History of Indiana from Its Earliest Exploration by Europeans to the Close of the Territorial Government in 1816: Comprehending a History of the Discovery, Settlement, and Civil and Military Affairs of the Territory of the U.S. Northwest of the River Ohio, and a General View of the Progress of Public Affairs in Indiana from 1816 to 1856.* Indianapolis: Bingham and Doughty, 1859.

———. *The National Decline of the Miami Indians.* Indiana Historical Society Publications, vol. 1. Indianapolis: Indiana Historical Society, 1897.

Dippie, Brian W. *The Vanishing American: White Attitudes and U.S. Indian Policy* (Lawrence: University Press of Kansas, 1991.

Doerr, Brian M. "The Massacre at Deer Lick Creek, Madison County, Indiana, 1824." *Indiana Magazine of History* 93 (March 1997): 19–47.

Dunn, Jacob Piatt, Jr. *Greater Indianapolis: The History, the Industries, the Institutions, and the People of a City of Homes.* Chicago: Lewis Publishing, 1910.

———. "The Moravian Mission Near Anderson." *Indiana Magazine of History* 9 (June 1913): 73–83.

Edmunds, R. David. "Justice on a Changing Frontier: Deer Lick Creek, 1824–1825." *Indiana Magazine of History* 93 (March 1997): 48–52.

———. *The Potawatomis: Keepers of the Fire.* Norman: University of Oklahoma Press, 1978.

Esarey, Logan. *History of Indiana from Its Exploration to 1922.* Dayton, OH: Dayton Historical Publishing, 1924.

————. *Indiana Home.* Bloomington: Indiana University Press, 1976.

————, ed. *Messages and Letters of William Henry Harrison.* 2 vols. Indianapolis: Indiana Historical Commission, 1922.

————. "Pioneer Politics." *Indiana Magazine of History* 13 (June 1917): 97–128.

Ewbank, Louis B. "Building a Pioneer Home." *Indiana Magazine of History* 40 (June 1944): 111–28.

Ferguson, Roger James. "The White River Indiana Delawares: An Ethnohistoric Synthesis." PhD diss., Ball State University, 1972.

Finley, James Bradley. *Life among the Indians; or, Personal Reminiscences and Historical Incidents Illustrative of Indian Life and Character.* Cincinnati: Curts and Jennings, [1875].

Forkner, John L. *History of Madison County Indiana: A Narrative Account of Its Historical Progress, Its People, and Its Principal Interests.* Chicago: Lewis Publishing, 1914.

Funk, Arville L. *Sketchbook of Indiana History.* Rochester, IN. Christian Book Press, 1969.

Gall, John F., and David K. Webb. *The Massacre of the Wigton Family, with an Account of the Trial of Samuel Mohawk, the Murder.* Chillicothe, OH: Privately Printed, 1936.

Gatch, W. D. "The Health of Our Poineer Ancestors." In *Indiana Pioneer Stories*, vol. 1. Edited by Doris Leistner. (New Albany, IN: D. Leistner, 2002), 310–20.

Gernhardt, Phyllis. "'Justice and Public Policy': Indian Trade, Treaties, and Removal from Northern Indiana, 1826–1846." In *The Boundaries between Us: Natives and Newcomers along the Frontiers of the Old Northwest Territory, 1750–1850.* Edited by Daniel P. Barr. Kent, OH: Kent State University Press, 2006).

Gipson, Lawrence Henry. *The Moravian Indian Mission on White River.* Indianapolis: Indiana Historical Bureau, 1938.

Harden, Samuel. *History of Madison County, Indiana from 1820 to 1874.* Markleville, IN, 1874.

Hauser, Susan Carol. *Sugartime: The Hidden Pleasures of Making Maple Syrup with a Primer for the Novice Sugarer.* New York: Lyons Press, 1997.

Heiss, Willard, ed. *1820 Federal Census for Indiana.* Indianapolis: Indiana Historical Society, 1966.

————, and R. Thomas Mayhill, eds. *Census of 1807, Butler County, Ohio.* Knightstown, IN: Eastern Indiana Publishing Company, 1968.

Helm, T. B., ed. *History of Hamilton County, Indiana, with Illustrations and Biographical Sketches of Some of Its Prominent Men and Pioneers.* Chicago: Kingman Brothers, 1880.

————, ed. *History of Madison County, Indiana, with Illustrations and Biographical Sketches of Some of Its Prominent Men and Pioneers.* Chicago: Kingman Brothers, 1880.

Hill, Frederick Dinsmore. "William Hendricks: Indiana Politician and Western Advocate, 1812–1859." PhD diss., Indiana University, 1972.

Hurt, R. Douglas. *The Indian Frontier, 1763–1846.* Albuquerque: University of New Mexico Press, 2002.

Johnston, Charles. "A Narrative of the Incidents Attending the Capture, Detention and Ransom of Charles Johnston." In *Held Captive by Indians: Selected Narratives, 1642–1836.* Edited by Richard VanDerBeets. Knoxville: University of Tennessee Press, 1972.

Johnston, John. "Recollections of Sixty Years." In *John Johnston and the Indians in the Land of the Three Miamis.* Edited by Leonard U. Hill. Piqua, OH: 1957.

Jordan, Philip D. "The Death of Nancy Hanks Lincoln." *Indiana Magazine of History* 40 (June 1944): 103–10.

Kappler, J. ed. *Indian Affairs: Laws and Treaties*. Vol. 2. Washington: Government Printing Office, 1904.

Larson, John Lauritz, and David G. Vanderstel. "Agent of Empire: William Conner on the Indiana Frontier, 1800–1855." *Indiana Magazine of History* 80 (December 1984): 301–28.

Latta, William C. *Outline History of Indiana Agriculture*. Lafayette, IN: Purdue University Press, 1938.

Lindley, Harlow, ed. *Indiana as Seen by Early Travelers: A Collection of Reprints from Books of Travel, Letters, and Diaries Prior to 1830*. Indianapolis: Indiana Historical Commission, 1916.

Linklater, Andro. *Measuring America: How Untamed Wilderness Shaped the United States and Fulfilled the Promise of Democracy*. New York: Walker and Company, 2002.

Madison, James M. *The Indiana Way: A State History*. Bloomington: Indiana University Press; Indianapolis: Indiana Historical Society, 1986.

Marks, Paula Mitchell. *In a Barren Land: The American Indian and the Quest for Cultural Survival, 1607 to the Present*. New York: Harper-Perennial, 2002.

Martin, John Bartlow. *Indiana: An Interpretation*. New York: Knopf, 1947.

Mazrim, Robert. *The Sangamo Frontier: History and Archaeology in the Shadow of Lincoln*. Chicago: University of Chicago Press, 2007.

McMurtry, Larry. *Oh What a Slaughter: Massacres in the American West, 1846–1890*. New York: Simon and Schuster, 2005.

Merrill, Boynton, Jr. *Jefferson's Nephews: A Frontier Tragedy*. Lincoln: University of Nebraska Press, 2004.

Modell, John. "Family and Fertility on the Indiana Frontier, 1820." *American Quarterly* 23 (December 1971): 615–34.

Netterville, J. J., ed. *Centennial History of Madison County Indiana: An Account of One Hundred Years of Progress, 1823–1923*. 2 vols. Anderson, IN: Historians' Association Publishers, 1925.

Nichols, Roger L. *Indians in the United States and Canada: A Comparative History*. Lincoln: University of Nebraska Press, 1998.

Nowland, John H. B. *Early Reminiscences of Indianapolis, with Short Biographical Sketches of Its Early Citizens, and a Few of the Prominent Business Men of the Present Day*. Indianapolis: Sentinel Book and Job Printing House, 1870.

———. *Sketches of Prominent Citizens of 1876, with a Few of the Pioneers of the City and County Who Have Passed Away*. Indianapolis: Tilford and Carlon, 1877).

Osborn, William M. *The Wild Frontier: Atrocities during the American-Indian War from Jamestown Colony to Wounded Knee*. New York: Random House, 2000.

Page, Jake. *In the Hands of the Great Spirit: The 20,000-Year History of American Indians*. New York: Simon and Schuster, 2003.

The Papers of John C. Calhoun. 28 vols. Columbia: University of South Carolina Press, 1959–2003.

Pence, George. "Phillip Sweetser and His Times." *Indiana Magazine of History* 23 (December 1927).

Phillips, Paul Chrisler. "The Fur Trade in the Maumee-Wabash Country." In *Studies in American History Dedicated to James Albert Woodburn*, vol. 12. Bloomington: Indiana University Studies, 1926).

Prucha, Francis Paul. *The Great Father: The United States Government and the American Indians*. Lincoln: University of Nebraska Press, 1984.

Rafert, Stewart. *The Miami Indians of Indiana: A Persistent People, 1654–1994*. Indianapolis: Indiana Historical Society, 1996.

Rayner, John A., ed. *The First Century of Piqua Ohio.* Piqua, OH: Magee Brothers, 1916.

Reid, Nina K. "James Noble." *Indiana Magazine of History* 9 (March 1913): 1–13.

Richter, Daniel K. *Facing East from Indian Country: A Native History of Early America.* Cambridge, MA: Harvard University Press, 2001.

Riker, Dorothy, ed. *Executive Proceedings of the State of Indiana, 1816–1836.* Indianapolis: Indiana Historical Bureau, 1947.

———, and Nellie Armstrong Robertson, eds. *The John Tipton Papers.* 3 vols. Indianapolis: Indiana Historical Bureau, 1942.

———, and Gayle Thornbrough, eds. *Messages and Papers Relating to the Administration of James Brown Ray, Governor of Indiana, 1825–1831.* Indianapolis: Indiana Historical Bureau, 1954.

Riley, James Whitcomb, *Little Orphant Annie and Other Poems.* Mineola, NY: Dover, 1994.

Silver, Peter. *Our Savage Neighbors: How Indian War Transformed Early America.* New York: Norton, 2007.

Smith, John C. *Reminiscences of Early Methodism in Indiana.* Indianapolis: J. M. Olcott, 1879.

Smith, O. H. *Early Indiana Trials and Sketches.* Cincinnati: Moore, Wilstach, Keys and Company, 1858.

Smith, W. L. G. *Fifty Years of Public Life: The Life and Times of Lewis Cass.* New York: Derby and Jackson, 1856.

Smith, William C. *Indiana Miscellany: Consisting of Sketches of Indian Life, the Early Settlement, Customs, and Hardships of the People, and the Introduction of the Gospel and Schools, Together with Biographical Notices of the Pioneer Methodist Preachers of the State.* Cincinnati: Poe and Hitchcock, 1867.

Spencer, Oliver M. *Indian Captivity: A True Narrative of the Capture of the Rev. O. M. Spencer by the Indians, in the Neighbourhood of Cincinnati.* 1835. Reprint, Ann Arbor, MI: University Microfilms, 1966.

Sulgrove, B. R., ed. *History of Indianapolis and Marion County, Indiana.* Philadelphia: L. H. Everts and Company, 1884.

Sweet, William Warren. *Circuit-Rider Days in Indiana.* Indianapolis: W. K. Stewart and Company, 1916.

Taylor, Colin F. *Native American Weapons.* Norman: University of Oklahoma Press, 2001.

Thompson, Charles N. *Sons of the Wilderness: John and William Conner.* Indianapolis: Indiana Historical Society, 1937.

Thompson, Maurice. *Stories of Indiana.* New York: American Book Company, 1898.

Tocqueville, Alexis de. *Democracy in America.* Vol. 1. Henry Reeve, trans. New Rochelle, NY: Arlington House, n.d.

Trigger, Bruce G., and Wilcomb E. Washburn, eds., *The Cambridge History of the Native Peoples of the Americas.* Vol. 1, *North America.* Cambridge: Cambridge University Press, 1996.

Trissal, Francis M. *Public Men of Indiana: A Political History.* Hammond, IN: G. B. Conkey, 1922.

Utley, Robert M. *The Indian Frontier of the American West, 1846–1890.* Albuquerque: University of New Mexico Press, 1984.

Viola, Herman J. *Thomas L. McKenney: Architect of America's Early Indian Policy, 1816–1830.* Chicago: Sage Books, 1974.

Waldman, Carl. *Who Was Who in Native American History.* New York: Facts on File, 1990.

Wallace, Anthony F. C. *The Death and Rebirth of the Seneca.* New York: Random House, 1972.

Wepler, William R. "Delaware Subsistence in East Central Indiana." In *Native American Cultures in Indiana: Proceedings of the First Minnetrista Council for Great Lakes Native American Studies.* Edited by Ronald Hicks. Muncie, IN: Minnetrista Cultural Center, 1992.

Wertz, J. A. *The Town of Pendleton, Together with a Sketch of Its Early History.* Anderson, IN: Brandon-Benham, 1896.

Weslager, Clinton Alfred. *The Delaware Indian Westward Migration.* Wallingford, PA: Middle Atlantic Press, 1978.

White, Richard. *"It's Your Misfortune and None of My Own": A History of the American West.* Norman: University of Oklahoma Press, 1991.

———. *The Middle Ground: Indians, Empires, and Republics in the Great Lakes Region, 1650–1815.* Cambridge: Cambridge University Press, 1991.

Woodburn, James Albert. "Local Life and Color in the New Purchase." *Indiana Magazine of History* 9 (December 1913): 210–23.

Woodworth, Samuel. *The Life and Confessions of James Hudson, Who Was Executed on Wednesday the 12th January, 1825, at the Falls of Fall Creek for the Murder of Logan, an Indian Chief of the Wyandott Nation.* Indianapolis: Printed at the Gazette Office for the author, 1825.

Woollen, William Wesley. *Biographical and Historical Sketches of Early Indiana.* Indianapolis: Hammond and Company, 1883.

Newspapers

Anderson Democrat.
Brookville Inquirer.
Evansville Gazette.
Indianapolis Gazette.
Indianapolis Journal.
Indianapolis Western Censor and Emigrants' Guide.
Madison Republican.
Pendleton Daily Register.
Pendleton Times.
Richmond Public Leger.
Salem Indiana Farmer.
Terre Haute Western Register.
Vincennes Western Sun.
Washington (NY) Republican and Congressional Examiner.

Index